MW01277093

World History:
No One Gets Out Alive

ISBN: 1500499447
ISBN-13: 978-1500499440

CONTENTS

CHAPTER 1: RUSSIA

The Romanov Imperial Family sitting for a portrait in 1913, by photographers Boissonas & Eggler.

The Romanov family was the last dynasty to rule Russia. Tsar Nicholas II is seated in the middle, to the left is his wife, Tsarina Alexandra, and at his feet is his son Alexei. His four daughters surround him. Four years after this photo was taken, the Bolshevik leadership ordered the family killed.

1.1 The Fall of the Romanovs

Nicholas II of Russia, painted by Lipgart.

In the late 1800's, where we'll begin our story, Russia was falling further and further behind its European neighbors. Once a great empire, Russia was now struggling to pay its bills. Previous tsars (kings) such as Alexander II had liberated the serfs, peasants who were bound to working the land and who lived a miserable existence. This action promised a brighter future for Russia's millions of landless poor, but his assassination in 1881 convinced his son, Alexander III, to restrict the freedom of the people significantly and move away from his father's populist stances.

When **Tsar Nicholas II** came to power in 1894, Russia was witnessing the Industrial Revolution unfolding in Britain, France, Germany and the United States. Russia, however, remained mostly farmland, unindustrialized and quickly falling behind. Russia also was caught up in growing tensions between neighboring countries.

Alas, Tsar Nicholas II made things even worse. He was an aloof and simple man, and did not understand what his people needed. His wife, the Tsarina Alexandra, had five children, including their youngest and only son, Alexei. This would in many ways be the undoing of the Romanov dynasty, which lasted over 300 years. Alexei had hemophilia, a rare disease often found in royal families where marriage to close family members could produce birth defects. Alexei's blood would not clot normally, and a simple paper cut or bruise could be deadly. The Tsarina (Queen) was devoted to her son, and tried everything to cure his condition. One day, she heard about a wandering religious healer by the name of **Rasputin** who had done wonders for another woman in her court. She summoned this mystery man to her court, where the piercing blue eyes of the mystic enthralled her. Surprisingly, Rasputin's methods were often able to relieve Alexei's pain and stop the bleeding. Recent research indicated this may be because royal doctors had always treated Alexei's pain with aspirin – widely known in the early 20th century to stop pain but not known for its anti-coagulant abilities. Banning all medical treatment (including aspirin) is believed to have been the secret to Rasputin's success.[1]

That does not sound like a good plan...   *Rasputin methods worked?!*

The Tsarina was grateful to the mystic—maybe a little too grateful. Historians believe a deeper relationship blossomed between the traveling preacher and the Tsarina, so much

Grigori Rasputin, the famous Russian mystic (1864-1916), author unknown, 1915.

so that when her husband was away, Rasputin moved into the palace and conducted official business! Rumors of infidelity in the court spread to advisors, aristocrats, and even outside the palace, further discrediting the royal family.

Those in the court became perturbed by this strange man and his undue rise to power. They plotted his murder. One night, he was lured to the home of the Tsar's niece. According to legend, several men poisoned his wine and cakes with enough cyanide to kill five men. When he carried on the conversation with not so much as a yawn, the men jumped out from their hiding places and beat him severely. Rasputin staggered away. Horrified that they might be caught, his pursuers grabbed a gun and fired at him, hitting him in the head. His assailants then threw Rasputin into the Neva River. He was found the next day. Suspected cause of death? Drowning. *It took so much to kill him*

Aside from wandering psychics invading the palace, the Tsar had another problem on his hands: his very own people. Several problems had appeared on the horizon: anger over the treatment of the peasants by the landlords, food shortages, and working conditions were paramount among them. *This was a bad plan*

Unfortunately, Tsar Nicholas II chose this moment to restore Russian pride by attacking Japan to seize Port Arthur, a desirable location in the Pacific Ocean that Russia had been leasing from Japan after its takeover of Korea.

Tsar Nicholas, going against the advice of all of his military advisors, presumed Japan could not defeat the Russian navy.[2] He was very, very wrong.

The Russo-Japanese War of 1904-1905 was a humiliating defeat for Russia and a signal to the rest of the world not to mess with Japan. Tsar Nicholas' troops were so ill-prepared for this battle that on one of their three battleships, a brutal mutiny broke out that would have repercussions far beyond this war.

The **Potemkin Mutiny** began when the second in command on the ship threatened to punish any crew members who did not eat the maggot-infested meat they were served that day. The crew members were marched towards their execution—they then turned on their superiors and killed seven of the eighteen officers on board. The ship docked in Romania where many of the leaders of the revolutionary group disembarked. Some of the ringleaders who returned to

The aftermath of Bloody Sunday, 1905.

Russia were executed for treason. This event had the effect of organizing a revolutionary army, and **Vladimir Lenin,** the first leader of the Soviet Union, considered it a "dress rehearsal" for the communist revolution that would come twelve years later.[3]

Kind of like the Texas-Mex war →Civil War

The treatment of the soldiers was not much better than the treatment of those in the city, who were desperate for some improvement in the appalling working conditions. Strikes had led to a lack of electricity and newspapers for months. Led by Russian priest Father Gapon, protesters made their grievances heard in a march towards the Winter Palace on Sunday, January 22, 1905.

Confronted by the Imperial Guards at the six points of entry into the square, the priest led the crowd, many of whom carried religious signs, in a rendition of "God Save the Tsar!" It was not enough to convince the Imperial Guard of their peaceful intentions. Some fired warning shots into the air –this prompted other nervous guards to fire directly into the crowd. At Gapon's entry point, the Guard fired directly at him, hitting 40 people around him. Gapon was uninjured. At another entry point, protesters were slashed with swords. A cannon was even fired into the crowd.[4]

unnecessary rational–bad look for the czars

The peaceful protest of 120,000 workers became a symbol of all that was wrong with Imperial Russia and became known as **Bloody Sunday**. Tsar Nicholas II was not even at the Winter Palace, having gone to the countryside after dismissing the protests as nonthreatening.

The event, however, was a disaster for the Tsar. He was blamed for the 200 deaths and 800 injuries sustained in the incident and was forced to issue the October Manifesto, granting more rights to the people and setting up a **Duma** or parliament in which (theoretically) the people would have a say in the governing of their Mother Russia.

However, the Duma was a "Dummy" government. Any law passed could be vetoed by the Tsar. The people quickly caught on to this attempt at appeasement and many began to consider the unthinkable: overthrowing the Tsar.

Section One Questions

1. Why are Russians frustrated in the late 1800's? How did different groups of people react to these frustrations? Through protests, defiance, outsiders
   The Tsars made Russia a miserable place

2. Why did Bloody Sunday happen? Give at least three reasons.
   • The man fell off his horse   • people wanted to see Tsar   • unknown that it was peaceful

3. How did the Tsar's rule over Russia contribute to his downfall? In 2-3 paragraphs, explain how he fell from power, including the Potemkin Mutiny, Bloody Sunday, Rasputin, the Duma, and the Industrial Revolution.
   During the Ind. Rev, Nick

1.2 The Revolutionary Years

Joseph Stalin (not his real name) was born in Gori, Georgia, a country to the south of today's Russia that was annexed by Russia in the 1800's. His early life may provide some clues to his later behavior, so pay close attention.

J.W. STALIN
Foto 1894

Stalin as a young man, 1894.

Stalin was born to a cobbler (shoemaker) and was afflicted by smallpox as a young child, leaving his face pockmarked for the rest of his life. He was also in not one but two carriage accidents that permanently damaged his left arm. He was quite short (I hope you're drawing a good picture of him in your head). He earned a scholarship to a seminary, but never completed his studies. Some historians suggest he was expelled for missing his final exams: the official Soviet record says his involvement in anti-Imperial and anti-religious activities and circles led to his dismissal.[5] Seminary records say he simply couldn't pay his bills.

Either way, Stalin left the seminary and began reading the works of Vladimir Lenin, a **Marxist** revolutionary whose ideas about worker's rights and the overthrow of the Tsar deeply intrigued the young Stalin. He was also fascinated by Marx's idea that the **proletariats** (working or lower class) should be in charge, rather than the **bourgeoisie** (upper class). Marx advocated for the proletariats to overthrow the bourgeoisie and live in a society where all property is owned communally (rather than privately).

At age 25, Stalin joined Lenin's **Bolshevik** (BULL-SHA-VICK) party, which fought for the rights of the proletariat. He began participating in the illegal activities of the outlaw group, including the production and distribution

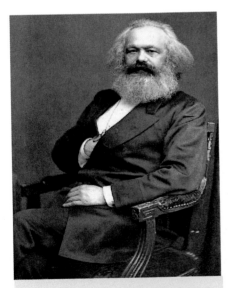

Karl Marx, portrait by John Mayall, 1875.

of propaganda, provoking strikes, and even leading bank robberies to secure the money necessary for the group's survival. For his activities, Stalin was exiled to Siberia seven times.[6] While there, he began writing down his Marxist ideas, and adopted the pen name Stalin, meaning Man of Steel (his real name was Ioseb Besarionis dze Jughashvili. Stalin is much simpler). But an event brewing back in St. Petersburg would soon have him breaking out of exile and taking on a new role entirely.

The February Revolution of 1917

Stalin and Lenin weren't the only ones seething at the ineptitude of the Imperial family. Back in St. Petersburg, Russians were witnessing blunder after blunder by their Tsar. His involvement in **World War I** worsened food shortages, and the supplies to the army had not improved since the disastrous Russo-Japanese War. These shortages compounded the already difficult conditions faced by the working class. The Tsar was entering his final days as ruler of Russia.

Bread riots (in which people are demanding bread) had engulfed St. Petersburg by February 1917, and strikers from most of the city's industrial plants poured into the streets. Women, children, students, and teachers all joined the workers in demanding that the Tsar make significant changes. The Tsar called on the army, but too few trained troops were left in the city to face the hundreds of thousands of protesters. Those who remained joined the protesters, and the city was now firmly in control of the people. The Tsar, on his way back to St. Petersburg, was stopped by a group of soldiers who had mutinied and was forced to abdicate (give up the throne). The **February Revolution** had been a success.

The Duma quickly set up a **Provisional Government** led by **Alexander Kerensky**. This government envisioned an end to the plight of the poor, but not in the way Lenin, Stalin, and the rest of the Bolsheviks were hoping for.

The Provisional Government was still comprised of mostly upper class aristocrats who believed Russia was not yet ready for **socialism** (in which the government, rather than private individuals, owns business, but goods and wages are unequal and based on work done).

The Bolsheviks, however, were more than ready for socialism. Their revolutionary newspaper, **Pravda** (meaning "Truth" in Russian) was critical of the pace of change of Kerensky's Provisional Government. The Bolshevik leaders began planning a second revolution, one that would introduce the world's first communist state.

The October Revolution, 1917

Vladimir Lenin, giving a speech to a Red Army gathering after taking over the government in 1920. Leon Trotsky is looking right at the camera. Stalin would later have Trotsky cropped out of the picture.

The newly formed government was weak and ineffective. It kept Russia in World War I despite repeated losses and the toll it took on the people back home. Protests encouraging the government to pull out of the war and end food shortages grew stronger. Meanwhile, Lenin was busy building loyalty amongst the army and the workers, creating **soviets**, or councils of workers, that gave the working people a sense of power they had never had before. With the help of talented writer **Leon Trotsky**, Lenin harnessed the tools of communication in Russia such as the telegraph lines, railroads, and newspapers. He simplified the message of Marx into the simple, and easily memorized slogan of "Peace, Land, Bread!"

After only eight months, the Provisional government found themselves surrounded on October 24 by a well-orchestrated assault of thousands of soviet workers and soldiers. In one day, the Winter Palace, headquarters of the government, fell under Lenin's control. The coup (takeover) was bloodless.[7]

With this tremendous success under his belt, Lenin summoned all of the soviets to St. Petersburg where he announced, "We shall now proceed to the construction of the communist order!" He followed through on this bold declaration by seizing all private property and outlawing the private ownership of land. Note that **communism** and socialism will frequently be used as synonyms. However, the banning of private property and unequal wages are two big differences between socialism and communism. Socialism allows for private property and unequal wages. Communism does not.

The state ownership of businesses and banks would begin gradually. Decrees in Russia went smoothly—including Lenin's order to execute the entire royal family, which had been living in exile in Siberia. Ending Russia's participation in the world's largest conflict to date, however, would prove more difficult.

The Treaty of Brest-Litovsk

Withdrawing from this conflict was easier said than done. Lenin agreed to surrender a large amount of Russian land and pay a large monetary penalty to their enemies, Germany and Austria-Hungary. In response to this forfeiture of land, Russia's already disenfranchised elite formed an organized opposition that drew many followers upset by the unfair treaty. This opposition group, called the Whites, grew into an armed resistance to the Bolsheviks (called the Reds) that would lead to the Russian **Civil War (1917-1923)** that further devastated the country.

A portrait of Leon Trotsky, published by Century Co, NY, 1921. Trotsky was Stalin's main rival, and was eventually exiled and killed at the hands of the KGB.

Leon Trotsky, a brilliant thinker, speaker, and intellectual, led the Bolsheviks' war effort. He maintained control of the railways and kept the Red Army well-supplied and morale high, while the White Army suffered from differing ideologies, poor organization, and weak morale.[8]

When the Civil War was over, Lenin proclaimed the official formation of the **Union of Soviet Socialist Republics** (USSR or Soviet Union for short), a federation of 15 states that were politically and economically dominated by the largest one, Russia. They included Armenia, Azerbaijan, Belarus, Estonia, Georgia, Kazakhstan, Kyrgyzstan, Latvia, Lithuania, Moldova, Russia, Tajikistan, Turkmenistan, Ukraine, and Uzbekistan. The Soviet Union would last from 1922 to 1991, maintaining an iron grip on all territories within it and implementing communism for the first time.

Lenin also set about removing any further threats to power through the **Red Terror**. The communist police, called the **Cheka**, interrogated, rounded up, and in many cases executed suspected political opponents. But Lenin would not be around long enough to enjoy his new unlimited power. He would suffer a series of debilitating strokes that would paralyze, and then end his life in 1924.

Section Two Questions

1. Describe Stalin's youth in depth.

2. Discuss the differences between the February Revolution and the October Revolution in three sentences. Which toppled the Tsar, and which brought the Bolsheviks to power?

3. The Bolsheviks' slogan was "Peace! Land! Bread!" Which parts of this promise do you think they fulfilled for the Russian people and why?

4. Why is Leon Trotsky significant? What roles did he play in the formation of the Soviet Union?

5. How is the Soviet Union (also called the USSR) different from Russia?

6. Describe Russia's Civil War. What were the two sides, and what was the outcome?

1.3 Stalin versus Trotsky

Lenin had not left plans for who should succeed him as the next premier (leader) of the Soviet Union, but there were two candidates who were eyeing the job before Lenin's body was even cold. Just a few months before Lenin died, Stalin became the Secretary-General of the Communist Party, which he transformed from a lowly administrative position into one of the most powerful seats in the party. With the power of appointment, Stalin created loyal supporters within the top ranks of the Communist Party. While Trotsky, the leader of the Red Army, gave impassioned speeches and won devoted followers from the common people, Stalin quietly plotted his rise behind closed doors.

Before Lenin died, he wrote that Stalin was "rude" and not to be trusted. He wrote that although Trotsky was arrogant, he would be the best choice to succeed him as leader. [9]

Unfortunately, these letters were never delivered to the right people. Stalin immediately began a campaign to convince members of the **Politburo** (the top committee in the Soviet Union) that Trotsky was a traitor and only Stalin could insure that communism continued in the right direction.

Stalin's behind the scenes work paid off. The Politburo began to turn against Trotsky, and he was expelled from the Politburo and then kicked out

Nikita Khrushchev and Joseph Stalin in 1936. Khrushchev would lead the Soviet Union following Stalin's death in 1953.

of the country completely. Stalin revealed his true colors then. He feared Trotsky was writing about him in exile, and sent his secret police to Mexico, where they killed Trotsky with an icepick to the back of the neck. Trotsky's fate would be shared by millions in the thirty years of Stalin's reign.

Man of Steel

Stalin began ambitious programs aimed to bring the Soviet Union up to speed with the rest of the industrialized world. In a series of **"Five Year Plans"**, the first of which began in 1928, the USSR's industrial output skyrocketed. Massive factories were built, and farmers were sent to the rapidly growing cities to work in them.

In order to compensate for a massive relocation of farmers from the countryside into the city, Stalin forced the remaining 25 million farmers into massive, state-run farms called collectives, where all materials, livestock, and labor were shared. Drought conditions and a decrease in productivity led the deaths of millions of people from this program. Agricultural output (how much the farms are producing) dropped sharply. Many Soviets began to wonder whether the industrial gains were worth such tragedies.

To prevent such talk, Stalin relied heavily on the internal police force, known as the **OGPU** (later known as the NKVD and then the **KGB**). Doubters were construed as "enemies" of the state. To hold the rapidly growing number of such enemies, large prison camps called **gulags** were built in the far regions of the country. Here prisoners toiled under terrible conditions. Some suspected "enemies" weren't so lucky. They were executed on the spot. The effect of the gulags was immediate—opposition was silenced and the fear of the government instilled in even the youngest of citizens.

To distance himself from the association with such terror, Stalin instituted a wide-ranging **propaganda** campaign. He constantly posed with children, many bringing him flowers or gifts, and distributed posters, newspapers, and flyers with these images throughout the country. The Pravda newspaper became the mouthpiece of the government, assuring Soviets that production was up, people were happy, and no one was getting killed by the government for opening their mouths. Stalin's use of propaganda was one of the many tools he used to prevent and silence dissent in the country.

Unfortunately, the gulags did not alleviate Stalin's belief that enemies of the state were everywhere. In 1934, he began the first purges, which shifted the spotlight from the common people into the top levels of the Soviet government. Top-ranking officials were accused of horrendous crimes, and put on **"show trials"** where the entire trial was orchestrated by the government to make the defendant look as guilty as possible.

The meeting of the Big Three: Winston Churchill of Britain, Franklin Roosevelt of the US, and Joseph Stalin at the Yalta Conference in 1945 to discuss Europe in the post-World War II era. National Archives.

Those accused of crimes they didn't commit were forced to admit to them and then were executed. When the ranks of the government were thoroughly decimated, the scope of the trials widened to include minor officials within the communist party and beyond. By the end of the **purges**, over a million people had been killed, and the Soviet Union was thoroughly controlled by one of the most despotic leaders the world has ever known.

Stalin vs. Hitler

To the rest of the world, it appeared that Stalin openly detested Germany and its leader, **Adolf Hitler**. However, with World War II looming on the horizon, Stalin and Hitler met in secret to sign the **German-Soviet Non-Aggression Pact,** in which the two powers agreed not to attack each other and instead to split Eastern Europe between them. This pact was broken, however, when Hitler attacked the Soviet Union during **Operation Barbarossa** in 1941.

The Soviet Union endured the most casualties of any country during the battles of World War II, but their refusal to lose to Germany and the harshness of the Russian winter aided in Germany's downfall. In 1945, when World War II ended with Europe in chaos, the Soviet Union was enjoying its place as one of two superpowers left in the world.

Section Three Questions

1. How did Stalin keep control over his population?

2. What happened in the Five Year Plan? What was a benefit? What were the problems?

3. What is a gulag? Who was sent there?

4. What was Stalin's relationship with Hitler?

5. Explain how Stalin changed Russia economically (how money was earned and distributed), politically (who was able to hold power), and socially (day-to-day life). Underline each change (there should be three minimum).

1.4 The Post-Stalin Era

Stalin died in 1953 from a heart attack, though some historians believe he may have been killed.[10] Either way, his death signaled the end of the most oppressive era of Russian government in history. When **Nikita Khrushchev** took power in 1958, he denounced many of the more extreme policies of the Stalin era. He also began to tangle with the world's other remaining superpower, the United States, intensifying the tensions of the **Cold War**. During his tenure, the **Space Race** was in full effect, with each country believing that space was the next frontier of war. The Soviets launched the world's first satellite, named **Sputnik**, causing panic in the United States that they were falling behind. In addition, the world came closer to nuclear war than ever before when tensions exploded over Cuba in October 1962 when Soviet warships were discovered bringing nuclear warheads to **Fidel Castro**, Cuba's communist leader. For twelve days, the world held its breath as it appeared that **President John F. Kennedy**'s options to avoid war were limited. After a **naval blockade**, Khrushchev eventually withdrew the missiles with JFK's promise to remove warheads pointing at the Soviet Union in Turkey.

Khrushchev was followed by **Leonid Brezhnev**, who returned to the more oppressive measures favored by Stalin. At first, he attempted to lessen tensions with the United States through **détente** (an easing of hostilities) but intensified them once more with the invasion of Afghanistan in 1979, an occupation that lasted ten years and created the Taliban. [11]

Gorbachev and the Collapse

In 1985, **Mikhail Gorbachev**'s election signaled the beginning of the collapse of the Soviet Union. He introduced policies of **perestroika** (an increase in economic freedom) and **glasnost** (an increase in political freedom) that allowed criticism of the Soviet regime for the first time in Soviet history.

Gorbachev, RIAN archive, 1986.

17

The fall of the **Berlin Wall** in 1989 prompted other eastern European nations under Soviet control to begin to demand their own free elections and an end to Soviet control. Amazingly, Gorbachev offered them the option to stay with the Soviet Union or leave, and when all chose to go, he did not pursue them with military action. For Gorbachev, the writing was on the wall. While on vacation in Southern Russia, he was notified that he had been removed from power in a coup by devoted communists. Though the coup ultimately failed, Gorbachev resigned as head of the Soviet Union in 1991, and allowed new leadership to take hold in the new Russia. The fifteen republics that were part of the union became independent, including Armenia, Azerbaijan, Belarus, Estonia, Georgia, Kazakhstan, Kyrgyzstan, Latvia, Lithuania, Moldova, Russia, Tajikistan, Turkmenistan, Ukraine, and Uzbekistan.

Putin - Medvedev - And Then Putin Again!

Despite the collapse of the Soviet Union, many institutions survive. The former head of the successor to the KGB, **Vladimir Putin**, became President in 2000 and served until 2008. He assumed the role of Prime Minister from 2008-2012 under **Dmitri Medvedev** before returning to the mantle of President in 2012. Many observers criticized the election that brought Putin back to power,

Vladimir Putin, 2006, Russian Presidential Press and Information Office.

which was widely believed to be fraudulent.[12] Basic political freedoms continue to be limited, and though the purges and gulags of the Stalin era no longer terrify the public, Russia still has a long way to go before it can claim to be a liberal democracy.

In 2014, a new crisis unfolded between Ukraine and Russia. When popular protests unseated Ukraine's pro-Russian President in January of 2014, Russia reacted by forcefully annexing the Ukranian region of Crimea, and then arming pro-Russian rebels in Eastern Ukraine. The international community was hesitant to get too involved, even after the passenger jet that was shot down while flying over Ukraine on July 17, 2014.

Seven leading intelligence agencies in the USA concluded in a January 2017 report that there was Russian meddling in the 2016 US Presidential elections, directly approved by President Putin.[13] This campaign to influence US elections continues to be of great concern to the United States intelligence community as some historians question whether the US is looking at the dawn of a new Cold War with Russia.

Putin won his fourth term in office in 2018. In January 2020, he proposed a vote to change the Constitution so that he could continue as President for two more six year terms. In July of 2020, this referendum passed with 78% voting yes, but also with reports of widespread voting irregularities and fraud.

Section Four Questions

1. Why did the Soviet Union collapse in 1991? Give at least three hypotheses.

2. Draw a chart comparing Khrushchev, Gorbachev, Brezhnev and Putin. Put them in chronological order, list each man's name, and one important thing about him or Russia (the Soviet Union) at the time.

3. Compare Putin's rule with Stalin's. How are they different? How are they the same?

CHAPTER 2: AFRICA

A lonely African Christian church in the Langa township, a remnant of apartheid. South Africa, 2012.

Fifty-four countries (including the world's newest, Southern Sudan) make up the continent of Africa. From deserts to waterfalls to lush tropical forests, the geographic diversity is reflected in the diversity of its people, its religions, its culture, and its history. All of Africa's countries have one common thread: their occupation by foreign powers that has lasting effects which continue to impact Africa today. We'll explore those effects in this chapter.

2.1 Africa's Pre-History

Pre-History is what historians call everything that happened before any of it could be written down. Evidence of what happened during this period comes from bones, tools, pottery, buildings and animal remains. What is most important to note about Africa's Pre-History is that this is the continent where humans first evolved from the great apes. This happened in many stages over millions of years. The scientific name of humans today is **Homo Sapiens**, which were thought to have first evolved between 100,000 and 150,000 years ago. What distinguishes Homo Sapiens from earlier evolutions is speech, which is why Homo Sapiens translates to 'wise man'. These wise men are thought to have first left their base in East Africa and migrated off the continent around 40,000 years ago. Considering the earth is thought to be some 4.6 billion years old, we are a relatively new player in the game of life on earth.

Behold King Tut Ankh Amun's famous Golden Funeral Mask. Photo by Steve Evans, 2005.

The Rosetta Stone

For many years, few Western historians placed any emphasis on the history of Africa. Written texts from Ancient Greece, China, and India provided a basis for the study of these cultures and their intricate histories. However, in many parts of Africa, particularly in Sub-Saharan Africa, these histories were passed down orally, from one generation to another, preserving the history within the society, but also keeping it from the reach of historians in other places in the world. This is one reason why the history of Africa often focuses greatly on the history of Egypt, for which historians now have a number of written texts to draw from.

In Ancient Egypt, people wrote in **hieroglyphics**, in which pictures represented words. This language was indecipherable to anthropologists and archaeologists until a massive stone was unearthed in 1799 by a band of French troops. The stone, found near the town of Rosetta, contained a law written in 196 BCE in three different languages that reflect the exchange of culture and language between Greece and Egypt.

The law was written in hieroglyphics, ancient Greek, and a more modern form of Greek. After 20 years of work, a French scholar was able to translate the hieroglyphics based on knowledge of ancient Greek. This decoding allowed future scholars to read a huge number of ancient Egyptian hieroglyphics that revealed to them a series of building blocks with which they could put together the history of Egypt for readers like you and me.

A photo of the Rosetta Stone by Hans Hillewaert. The actual stone is housed in the British Museum, even though it's Egyptian.

Ancient Egypt

The Egyptians believed their pharaoh was both a god and a monarch (king or queen). The pharaoh was the Egyptians' link to the afterlife, so they took particular care in preserving their bodies as mummies ~ and no, not with toilet paper like you did that one time for Halloween.

Mummification was an expensive and time-consuming process reserved only for the pharaoh or the very rich. The body was sliced down the side to remove the intestines, liver, stomach, and lungs. The organs were then wrapped in linen and stored in jars. The brain was removed through the nose using long hooks. They believed that the brain was not useful and so they often discarded it.[14] Oops.

The body was stuffed for 40 days to drain any fluids.[15] After the stuffing was removed, the body was very dry, and had shrunken significantly . The body was once more stuffed with packing and covered in jewels - and then wrapped in about 20 layers of linen. Due to this process, we were able to recover the body of and learn about the pharaoh **Menes** ("meanies"), the first known pharaoh of Egypt. Menes united two kingdoms, called Lower Egypt and Upper Egypt and established what we now call the "Old Kingdom" about 3100BC.

This is what he's famous for ~ that and being mauled to death by a hippopotamus.[16] Yikes.

King Tut

Tutankhamen, the "boy king" never became a "man king"~ because he died at age 19. His death was long a mystery, and most of the treasures of the pyramids were plundered.

One painter's vision of the savvy Cleopatra.
John William Waterhouse, 1888.

However, by accident Tutankhamen's tomb remained intact because it was buried by rock chips dumped from the cutting of a tomb of a later pharaoh. The tomb lay hidden for more than 3,000 years until an archaeologist discovered it in 1922. His discovery made "King Tut" and his buried treasures famous, and revealed to archaeologists a massive trove of information about how the Egyptians lived~and died.

Cleopatra, Coming At Ya

Alexander the Great was a Greek military genius, renowned for never losing a battle and creating one of the world's largest empires. He led his army into Egypt and freed the Egyptian people from Persian rule, which was tyrannical by all accounts. The grateful Egyptian people worshipped Alexander as a pharaoh and a liberator.

Alexander's vast empire was divided among his top generals when he died in 336 BCE. Ptolemy, a former general became the ruler of Egypt and the first ruler of the Ptolemic dynasty. Ptolemy XII's daughter **Cleopatra**, however, is the one who would make history a lot more interesting.

Cleopatra's life is a story of love, greed, and romance. It also serves to explain the overlap of Greek and Egyptian history, as her life fell right in the thick of it. She was born in 69 BCE, after the era of the pharaohs had passed, but some in her kingdom worshipped her anyways. Though Cleopatra was born in Egypt, her ancestry was Greek.

When Ptolemy XII died in 51 BCE, he willed that Cleopatra (age 17) and her brother, Ptolemy XIII (age 12), were to marry and rule Egypt. This was a lot more common than you think~it was a way to ensure power remained within the family.

Cleopatra was a very different ruler than the Ptolemies who came before her. She learned the Egyptian language; other Ptolemies spoke only Greek. Cleopatra practiced the religious customs of Egypt, and many of the Egyptians viewed her as a pharaoh. In 48 BCE, Cleopatra's generals found they couldn't control her, so they ousted Cleopatra and made her brother the sole monarch of Egypt.

But Cleopatra wasn't going to quit that easily. A few months later, a Roman army led by **Julius Caesar** arrived in Egypt. Caesar was pursuing another Roman army that tried to keep him from returning to Rome. Caesar's army was much larger than the Egyptian forces, so Cleopatra concluded that Caesar could return her to power.

She arranged to have a huge carpet delivered to the 52-year-old Caesar. When he unrolled it, he found the 22-year-old former queen wrapped inside[17] . Caesar and Cleopatra became lovers, and the Roman general led his army to capture and kill the people who removed her from power. Ptolemy XIII (her younger brother) drowned in the Nile while trying to flee.

Egyptian law did not allow a queen to rule without a king, so Cleopatra married another younger brother, Ptolemy XIV. Despite the marriage, she remained deeply in love with Caesar.

Caesar and Cleopatra spent the next several months traveling along the Nile, where Caesar saw how the Egyptian people worshipped Cleopatra. Caesar was a very powerful general who conquered many lands, but he knew that becoming a pharaoh was something he could not ever achieve.

But then in 44 BCE... CAESAR WAS MURDERED!

Rome was in turmoil after Caesar's murder. Several armies competed for control. The two greatest were those of **Marc Antony** and **Octavian**. Octavian was the adopted son of Julius Caesar, but Marc Antony was believed to have led a larger army.

When Antony asked Cleopatra to meet with him, Cleopatra decided that she had another opportunity to return to power both in Egypt and in Rome. A legend says that Cleopatra adorned her ship with so many rose petals that the Romans knew of her fragrance before they could see her ship.

Cleopatra walked off the ship dressed as Aphrodite, the Greek goddess of love.[18] Antony was immediately love-struck with the Egyptian queen. Antony was already married to Octavian's sister, but he took Cleopatra as his wife and had two children.

Octavian's army defeated Marc Antony's forces and led an invasion of Egypt in 31 BCE. Antony committed suicide by falling on his sword.

Fearing that she would be forced to live as a slave in the land she once ruled, Cleo decided it would be better to end her life. According to legend, the former queen asked that an asp, an Egyptian cobra, be delivered to her in a basket of figs. The asp was a symbol of divine royalty to the Egyptians, so by allowing the asp to bite her, Cleopatra is said to have become immortal. However, in recent years several scholars of Ancient Egypt have questioned the validity of this romantic, but unlikely legend. These scholars believe it is more likely that Cleopatra, with a proven knowledge of poisons and of how unlikely an asp bite was to kill you would have chosen poison instead.[19]

Section One Questions

1. What is the importance of the Rosetta Stone? Can you think of any modern-day "Rosetta Stones" (tools used to translate languages)?

2. How did Cleopatra become so powerful? Suggest three possible reasons and defend them.

3. Consider the mummies. What five artifacts do you think would give archeologists living 1,000 years in the future the greatest amount of information about human life today?

The history of Ancient Egypt has fascinated historians as well as students for their intricate mummification process, wild pharaoh drama, pyramids, and celebrated place in the Bible as the birthplace of Moses. But the history of Ancient Egypt does not speak for the rest of Ancient Africa at all. There were large, prosperous kingdoms all over the Western coast of Africa, that benefited from enormous and wealthy trading empires.

One of the earliest and most well-known Western African empires was that of **Ghana**. Ghana lasted from the 4th century CE up until 1050 CE and prospered by taxing the trade from Northern Africa to the Western Coast. In particular, they were a large part of both the salt and gold trade.

The empire of **Mali**, for example, was so wealthy, that its king, **Mansa Musa**, once took a pilgrimage to Mecca, in modern-day Saudi Arabia, and spent most of the trek throwing gold to the civilians he passed in countries along the way. In Cairo, where he made his most famous stop, the amount of gold Mansa Musa threw into the streets lowered the price of gold for 12 years. [20] His travels were recorded by the Moroccan traveler Ibn Battuta, who also visited and wrote about such far off lands as China, Indonesia, India, Eastern Africa, and Sri Lanka.

Mansa Musa, as drawn by Abraham Cresques in the Catalan Atlas in 1375.

Mali was succeeded by the kingdom of **Songhay**, which is famous for its city of scholarship, **Timbuktu**. At its height, Timbuktu was a university serving 25,000 students. Scholars came from thousands of miles away to learn from professors who taught mathematics, astronomy, literature, and physics.

Other kingdoms included the forest kingdom of Benin and the kingdom of Dahomey with its famous units of all-female warriors.

Influence of Islam

We will spend a significant amount of time talking about Islam in our chapter on the Middle East, but the world's second largest religion has a huge role in the history of the African continent as well. The religion began in Saudi Arabia in the 7th Century CE and made its way to North Africa through Muslim conquerors by 711 CE. Timbuktu was its intellectual hub, but the religion spread quickly not only through the empires and villages of the North but also in the West. Today there is a significant split between the North, which is predominantly Muslim, and the South, which is a mix of Christian, animist, and Muslim.

Zimbabwe & Swahili

To the South, the largest recorded empire was that of the **Zimbabwe**, which means "great stone house". The Zimbabwe were known, not surprisingly, for their massive stone structures, some of which survive today and which early European explorers doubted could be the work of Africans.[21] The Zimbabwe enriched themselves through the trade of ivory, gold, and copper.

The Zimbabwe traded with the Swahili people who lived in independent city-states along about 1,000 miles of the coast of East Africa. Their cities competed for dominance in trading the desirable African goods of gold, ivory, and timber, and receiving textiles from India and porcelain from China. The Swahili developed a distinctive culture that blended these influences, adopting Arabic phrases and the religion of Islam. Ibn Battuta also got around to visiting the Swahili empire (because that guy went EVERYWHERE) and observed the unique trade routes that truly made this East African coastline an international trading hub.

The traders living on the Swahili Coast had some of the first encounters with the Portuguese, whose arrival in South Africa in 1497 would change the lives of Africans forever.

Section Two Questions

1. What does the story of Mansa Musa reveal about the Mali empire? What does the story of the Zimbabwe reveal about their empire?

2. Briefly explain how Islam spread to Africa and brainstorm two reasons it may have spread so quickly.

2.3 The Cape of Hopeful Storms

In the 15th century, there was a race to discover new lands, new routes, new markets, and new riches for the competing empires of Europe. This period was called the Age of Exploration, and marked the end of Africa's independence and relative isolation from Europe.

The Portuguese were the first to successfully find a water route from Portugal around Africa to India. This route was theoretically much cheaper and faster than the water-land-water route previously used to go from Europe to Asia. In 1488, explorer Bartholemeu Dias arrived at the Southwesternmost tip of Africa. Around the point, he experienced terrible storms and sailing conditions, prompting him to name it "the Cape of Storms" and to turn around after his crew began to threaten to mutiny.[22]

This title was a bit too discouraging for the King of Portugal, who chose to rename it the "Cape of Good Hope" in the belief that more sailors would sign on to round the Cape of Good Hope than the foreboding "Storms"[23]. He was right. In 1497, Vasco da Gama was the first to lead a successful European expedition around the tip of Africa and reach India.

Da Gama hoped to set up a refueling post in the Eastern Cape, but immediately realized the error of this view. The **Xhosa** (also spelled Khosa) people who lived in the area viewed the Portuguese as a threat, and spent years trying to drive them out of their native land. The Portuguese eventually abandoned the idea of a refueling port, and the Xhosa would be free from intervention ~ until the arrival of the Dutch 100 years later.

The Dutch East India Company

The Portuguese were quickly followed by the Dutch, who set up a trading company specializing in the Europe-India market, and, like the Portuguese, eyed the eastern Cape area for a refueling station. The Xhosa people were more willing to trade and sell goods to the Dutch, and an uneasy trading relationship emerged.

In addition to buying meat from the Xhosa and selling them copper, beads, iron, and tobacco, the Dutch set up a hospital for sick sailors and grew fruits and vegetables to help the sailors ward off scurvy. Soon the Dutch were looking to expand their farms that supplied them with this produce, and they looked to the flat grazing lands owned by the Xhosa to fulfill this need.

The Xhosa were not going to relinquish these lands without a fight. The first of the Dutch-Xhosa wars was fought in 1659, and though there was no obvious winner, the Dutch declared they had the "right of conquest" over the entire cape.[24] Conflicts between the Xhosa and the Dutch raged as the colony on the cape expanded. More Dutch arrived, becoming farmers (called **Boers** by the Dutch) and also pastoralists (those who herd animals).

By the 19th century, the Dutch had conquered most of the Xhosa territory and even expanded north into more sparsely populated areas. They no longer called themselves Boers, but **Afrikaners**, after the dialect of Dutch, Afrikaans, that they spoke.

In 1795, the British seized the Cape colony from the Dutch. The British found the Afrikaners, whom they still called the Boers, to be a real pain in their side. Conflicts between the two groups for territory erupted in a series of British-Boer wars, which ended in Boer defeat in 1901. Although the British military might have ended up crushing the Afrikaners, the British figured that it would be less work for them if they acquiesced to the Afrikaner request that the country of South Africa be under white rule--both British and Afrikaner.

A painting depicting a Boer (Dutch farmer) camp being attacked by Zulus in South Africa. Painted by Charles Bell, 1838.

Black South Africans were excluded from all levels of government and brutally discriminated against for the next 93 years.

The Fatal Hunt for the Source of the Nile

As more and more delegations of European explorers arrived in Africa, fewer and fewer mysteries remained unsolved. Most of the exploration and conquest was occurring on the coastlines, where ports could be established and goods could be shipped in and out, or supplies restocked.

One mystery that many European countries wished to solve was the source of the world's longest and Africa's most important river, the Nile. Running 4,160 miles north through

A photo of Richard Francis Burton from Men of Mark, 1876. The scar below his eye is from a spear thrown through his face by Somali tribesmen.

Uganda, Sudan, and Egypt, it feeds and supports millions of Africa's inhabitants. Control of the source of the Nile meant control of these countries and all those supported by it. Britain was foremost among the countries searching for the source, and put by far the most resources into its discovery. [25]

Two famed explorers named **John Speke** and **Richard Burton** were tasked with its discovery in the mid 1800's. The journey would not be an easy one.

At first, Speke and Burton formed a dynamic team, but midway through their first attempt in Africa, they were attacked by a Somali tribe that launched a spear through Burton's cheek

John Speke by Samuel Hollyer, based on a Southwell Brothers Photograph, 1864.

The famous explorer Dr. David Livingstone. Portrait by Thomas Annan, 1896.

and captured and knifed Speke. Both men were able to escape and recover back in Europe, but somehow, they were willing to go back for more.

On their second trip together, Speke felt a beetle crawl into his ear. As one might expect when a knife is in one's ear, Speke's attempt to remove the beetle rendered him deaf. He also temporarily went blind from malnutrition. Burton was not immune either. He fell gravely ill, and could not continue on. Speke was undeterred. He remembered that Burton had expressed a wish to go North to a body of water Arab traders had told the two about and went alone, leaving Burton near death. When he reached the lake, he proclaimed it the source and named it for Queen Victoria. He rushed back home, breaking an agreement to present on the source together. [26]

Once both men had their feet firmly planted on British soil, a debate was planned in which the men were expected to present their evidence for having found the legitimate source of the Nile.

The morning before the debate was slated to begin, however, Speke went on a hunt and never returned. He had shot himself. The coroner ruled his death an accident but some historians believe that he was worried about the lack of evidence he had to back up his claim--and how determined Burton was to slander his old friend's name as revenge for abandoning him in Africa.

Looking for Evidence: Dr. Livingstone and Henry Stanley

Dr. **David Livingstone** is perhaps the most famous of all the European explorers of Africa. A

A caricature of Henry Morton Stanley, by Frederick Waddy, 1872.

missionary doctor, he traversed Central Africa in both directions and crossed the Kalahari desert. During his 24 years of travel by foot from 1841 to 1873 (with a few stops back in England), he documented the Zambezi River and the famous Victoria Falls, which he named for Britain's queen.

He encountered native people whom he treated with respect and courtesy and wrote extensively about~unlike almost every other explorer of his time. He also met slave traders, and his accounts of their activities helped end the practice in England.[27]

During his final adventures in Africa, Livingstone was trying desperately to confirm or deny the reports that Speke had delivered of Lake Victoria as the source of the Nile.

Near the end of his adventure, his health deteriorated significantly. After a disturbingly long period without any contact, a young American reporter named **Henry Morton Stanley**, who had never been to Africa, was sent to find him and return him to Britain~and report back all the juicy details for the *New York Herald* newspaper.

After two years, Stanley found Livingstone clinging to life in the village of Ujiji near Lake Tanganyika, and, according to his own journals, asked the man he had been searching for for years this question: "Dr. Livingstone, I presume?" Livingstone was (again, by Stanley's account) overjoyed to see him but refused to return to England with Stanley and Stanley was forced to return to England with Livingstone's diaries and letters, but without the man himself. Livingstone died a year later, and his body is buried in Westminster Abbey, though, upon his request, his heart was buried in Africa.

King Leopold II by Jef Leempoela, 1905 .

Stanley was by then bitten by the traveling bug, and continued his travels in southern Africa, charting Lake Victoria and many other landmarks previously unknown to those outside of Africa. He later would claim a huge chunk of Central Africa for a man who would do terrible things to its people: **King Leopold II.**

Three G's vs. Three C's

Early explorers went to Africa for three main reasons: Gold, Glory, and God. Those seeking gold were tantalized by stories like that of Mansa Musa, and promises of riches from anxious kings and queens in Europe. Those seeking glory took a page from Vasco da Gama, celebrated for his feat of pioneering a route from Europe to India. Finally, there were those like David Livingstone who followed the call of God and believed that the word must be spread to the "Dark Continent" which had not yet been exposed to the words of the Bible.

As more and more ports were established, Commerce, Civilization and Christianity (the **Three C's**, if you will) became the focus of these trips to Africa. There were rubber trees to harvest, fruits and spices to collect and sell back in Europe, metals to mine, and labor to exploit. Amongst Europeans, a deep racism drove their actions on the continent.

The first step towards lightening

The White Man's Burden

is through teaching the virtues of cleanliness.

Pears' Soap

is a potent factor in brightening the dark corners of the earth as civilization advances, while amongst the cultured of all nations it holds the highest place—it is the ideal toilet soap.

An ad in *The Cosmopolitan* in 1899 urges British citizens to bring soap and civilization to the "dark corners of the earth."

The beliefs about the Africans were that they were backward, unenlightened, and uncivilized. Many took it upon themselves to bring "Civilization" to this continent.

You will also notice from the 1899 advertisement above that soap was called "the first step towards lightening The White Man's Burden" which reflected the common belief in Europe that European exploration and settlement in Africa was a "burden" that whites must take upon themselves in order to bring a better civilization to the Africans.

The Three G's and Three C's give you an idea of why explorers, missionaries, and businessmen decided to embark on the journey to the African continent. Their intentions were not necessarily to cause war, spread disease, or devastate local economies. But many of their actions, unfortunately, would lead to these outcomes for generations to come.

Section Three Questions

1. How was the Cape of Good Hope "discovered" for the first time by Europeans, and by whom?

2. Describe the relationship between the Dutch East India Company and the Xhosa people.

3. Why was discovering the source of the Nile so important? What trials and tribulations did the explorers suffer in their quest?

4. What are the Three C's? What are the Three G's? Which one has to do with the White Man's Burden?

2.4 The Scramble for Africa

A sketch of the Berlin Conference by Adalbert von Roessler, 1884. Notice the Africa map in the back.

European powers wanted colonies in Africa for many reasons: among them were the need for raw materials and new markets created by the Industrial Revolution. Another was competition: fierce European nationalism meant the countries of Western Europe were in a hotly contested race to become the largest, richest, and strongest nation in Europe. Two forms of racism were used to justify the actions of the Europeans: the belief in the survival of the fittest race, known as Social Darwinism, and the belief that it was the White Man's Burden to take care of the Africans.

Others went for social and economic opportunities that they could not get back home. A continent full of unconverted souls meant a huge increase in missionary activity. The desire to be the dominant force in Europe led to the need for military and naval bases. Finally, as the Industrial Revolution drove population growth and urbanization, European countries were looking for places to dump their unwanted populations, such as criminals and the chronically poor. Whew. That's a lot of motivations to colonize, which might help you understand why so many countries felt they had to get in the game ~ before it was too late.

By the late 1800's, every country in Europe with the means to field an expedition had motivations to gain colonies in Africa, and tensions were rising among those already there. The leaders of these countries decided to come together in a "civilized" way to carve up what King Leopold II of Belgium referred to as "the magnificent African cake" once and for all.[28]

In 1884 local and traditional leaders still controlled 80% of the African continent. The conference was scheduled for Berlin, Germany, in 1884, and was to include fourteen Western European nations with eyes on Africa. Not one African was invited. The maps were out, and Africa's future was about to be decided by men who had never set foot there before.[29]

Direct vs. Indirect Rule

The nations gathered in Berlin drew boundaries that reflected their desire for waterways, ports, mines, and other advantages in the great imperial game. They did not consider ethnic rivalries, language differences, migration patterns, or previous claims to the land. The two countries which dominated the conference were Britain and France, whose navy and military superiority at the time gave them large tracts of land that spanned West to East (France) and north to south (Britain). Portugal was able to maintain the countries in which it had its largest ports. King Leopold of Belgium was able to maintain his personal playground in the Congo, while Spain, once a great colonial and naval power, now tried to secure a few small ports across the western coast. Germany, one of the later players in the game, received prime real estate near the mouth of the Congo river. Italy tried to take lands in North Africa, but would later fail to take Ethiopia, the one African country never successfully colonized by an outside power.

The United States even sent a delegation of ex-slaves to Liberia from the **American Colonization Society (ACS)**. The idea was to solve the conundrum in the United States about what to do with all the freed slaves ~ the ACS (and some freed slaves) believed the best solution was to send them to Africa ~ despite the fact that it was their ancestors mostly who had come from Africa, and that very few, if any, had come from Liberia. Freed slaves arriving in Liberia did not know the language, the culture, the climate, or the ways of the native Liberians. Many of the freed slaves, and their later descendants, ended up treating the locals terribly, and set Liberia up for a massive civil war at the end of the 20th century between descendants of the freed slaves and the natives.

Once boundaries were drawn, the business of colonizing began. There were two main schools of thought: one believed that to effectively rule another country, the mother country had to develop and train a local elite to do much of the governing for them. Often this came in the form of local chiefs and rulers, who were co-opted by the British to rule the way the British wanted. This was the angle the British adopted, which became known as **indirect rule**.

The other method of colonizing was **direct rule**, in which officials from the mother country (in this case, France) ruled their subjects without any local leadership or assistance. A third type of rule, called settler rule, involved the mother country shipping hundreds and sometimes thousands of their citizens to the colony to settle it and rule it for the mother country. This occurred in the British colony of Kenya and the French colony of Algeria.

The French were also fans of **assimilation**, meaning that they imposed the French language, culture and customs on their colonies while simultaneously restricting or punishing use of the native culture.[30] They wanted their colonies to be extensions of France, which had lasting impacts on the people living there, even today.

Resistance and Rebellion

There was resistance to colonial rule in almost every country, but the scale of the resistance varied dramatically. From the beginnings of Britain's settlement in Kenya, the Kikuyu, Kenya's largest ethnic group, fought against the encroachment of the white settlers, who took the most fertile highlands, forced the Kikuyu to move from place to place, and often used them as labor in the production of cash crops.

Cash crops can be devastating to a local population because they are used solely for export and not for consumption (tobacco and cotton are two good examples), so if they fail, there is nothing to generate income and nothing to eat. No one can survive eating cotton and tobacco, after all.

The Kikuyu fought against the incursions and were finally able to mount a semi-successful resistance in the **Mau Mau Rebellion** of the 1950s, attacking and killing 32 white civilians.[31] The British retaliated by killing over 11,000 Kikuyu and imprisoning some 150,000 in poorly kept, disease-ridden labor camps, which one official referred to as concentration camps and "gulags" (you should remember this term from the gulags Stalin set up in the Soviet Union).

The withdrawal of the British in 1963 is said to have been in part due to this uprising, and the first elected President, **Jomo Kenyatta**, was a leading spokesman for the rebellion.

Ethiopia (called Abyssinia at the time) provides the most successful example of an African-led resistance. **Menelik II** was the emperor of the Ethiopians during the height of colonization in the late 1800's. Seeing the plight of his fellow Africans, Menelik II used the profits from the ivory industry in his country to begin a determined program of modernization in Ethiopia. He imported modern European weapons, brought in European experts to design and implement modern infrastructure (roads, schools, bridges) and even invited European military officers to train his army. Thus, when the Italians saw the last remaining independent country on the map of Africa and launched a war to colonize it, Menelik II and his army were ready. The Italian army was destroyed at the Battle of Adowa in 1896 and forced to retreat home to Europe. They would attempt to invade Ethiopia once more in 1935 with 100,000 troops, but, after dropping poisonous gas on the capital, would fail at that attempt too.

King Leopold II

One of the most brutal colonizations in the 1800's was in the heart of Africa, what is today the Democratic Republic of the Congo. King Leopold II of Belgium commissioned Henry Stanley (yes, the very same one) to claim a large swath of central Africa for Leopold to expand his kingdom and its source of materials. Through gifts and demonstrations of force, Stanley had illiterate chiefs all throughout the Congo sign over their land to the King. To secure his claim, King Leopold II went to America, then to the rest of his colonial competitors in Europe to ensure they recognized his claim to the massive Congo, an area 80 times that of Belgium, as legitimate.

In the Belgian Congo, King Leopold II developed a terrifying plantation of epic proportions. Through his hired army, he enslaved millions in the Congo to harvest rubber, which was exploding in value with the invention of the rubber inflatable bicycle tire and later with the automobile.

Congolese slaves worked in brutal conditions, and when they fell short of expectations, the punishment was often the cutting off of one's hand or holding the women hostage. If the overseers believed this punishment was unsuccessful, the children of workers were also subject to the same punishment.

Joseph Conrad, one of the 20th century's most famous authors, spent six months in the Congo in 1890, and his account of the cruelty in the Congo makes its way into the celebrated novel, *Heart of Darkness*. Reports by missionaries and colonial officials eventually leaked out of the Congo and in 1908, the Belgian parliament took the Congo away from King Leopold, who had used it as his own personal piggy bank for 24 years, accruing a fortune of $1.1 billion dollars, and forever scarring the heart of the continent.[32]

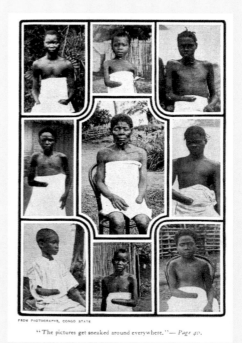

Portraits of victims of King Leopold's rubber plantations. From Mark Twain's King Leopold's Soliloquy, 1905.

Section Four Questions

1. Describe in depth the motives for the colonization of Africa.

2. What is the difference between indirect and direct rule?

3. Describe the devastation that King Leopold II brought upon the Congo. Brainstorm three ways the Congo may still be affected today.

2.5 Outside Pressures & Independence

In 1939, World War II broke out when Germany, ruled by Adolf Hitler, invaded Poland. Britain and France (and later the United States and the Soviet Union, forming what were called the **Allied** forces) declared war in response. Soon Europe, and by default her colonies, were in a full-scale international conflict that would command the attention of the world for the next six years.

The colonies in Africa were not immune from the crisis. They were heavily relied upon for supplies and hundreds of thousands of Africans from British colonies fought against the Japanese. The heavy racial discrimination prevented them from being officers in any division and in many cases, from fighting at all, but they participated as ground and air crews, in construction of bases, and in supplying Allied and **Axis** (Germany, Japan and Italy) troops in Europe.

Despite the Allied win, the British and French were decimated by the war. Facing huge debts and massive rebuilding in their own countries, which had been battlegrounds in the war, they could not maintain their presence in the colonies like before. Africans seeking independence saw this weakness as their moment of opportunity.

Many African independence seekers also took advantage of the growing tension (aka the Cold War) that began forming between the world's remaining two superpowers, the United States and the Soviet Union. The two powers, desperate to make sure any newly independent countries chose the right side, supported independence movements that aligned with their economic systems (capitalist allies with the United States, or communist allies with the Soviet Union). This led to a stream of weapons, military and financial support to groups seeking to overthrow their colonial rulers and replace them with African leadership.

The United States, newly minted as a world superpower, also discouraged the continuation of colonialism and heavily influenced the Europeans to withdraw from their remaining colonies in Africa.

Though only four African countries were independent in 1950, that was about to change dramatically. In the three decades following the end of World War II, nearly

40

all of Africa would transition to being under self-rule. But it would not be easy. Independence would come sometimes through brutal and bloody struggles. The vacuum of power left behind by the Europeans who had given no formal training to anyone in the colonies would lead to decades of corruption, coups and civil wars. In a few cases, the transition went peacefully, but problems of colonization lingered, such as in the divisions between ethnic groups who received better treatment and other groups, who were not so lucky.

Forces for Independence: Domestic Factors

While the problems of Europe certainly contributed to the end of colonial rule in Africa, a growing movement in much of Africa made a significant impact as well. That movement was **African nationalism**, and it was led by a group of educated and proud Africans who wanted to return to an "Africa for Africans."

Especially in the British colonies where indirect rule was used, an elite class of Africans was being groomed to assist in the ruling of the countries.

These elites would often be sent abroad for their schooling, and would return to Africa with the ideas of de-

Senegal's first President, Léopold Senghor. Roger Pic, 1975.

41

mocracy and self-rule that were in stark contrast to the reality of colonialism. These elites began to form groups that became even stronger after over one million African colonial subjects were forced to fight on behalf of their colonizers in World War I.[33]

In South Africa, this group became known as the **African National Congress** (ANC), which continues to be a powerful political party in the country today.

Another, broader movement called **Pan-Africanism** expanded beyond the borders of nationalism to encompass the continent. It emphasized that all Africans should be unified in their struggle against imperialism, and reached out to Africans living abroad as well. In addition, the negritude movement popularized by West African and Caribbean authors sought to elevate African heritage, culture, and pride and put a stop to the negative stereotypes of Africans perpetrated by Europeans. The most famous of these authors was **Leopold Senghor**, who would go on to lead Senegal's fight for independence and become its first elected president.

African nationalism was most successful as an independence movement in Egypt. Egypt had a long and proud history to rally around, and after experiencing hardship and sacrifice during World War I, strikes and protests forced Britain to leave in 1922, though Egypt's monarchy remained under their control.

A group called the **Muslim Brotherhood**, which rejected Western culture and influence, then became the unifying force for independence from this control. In 1952, a **coup d'etat** (overthrow of the government, generally by the military) replaced the British-controlled monarchy with a republic, and began a new chapter in Egypt's storied history. Coups such as this would remain a big part of Egypt's modern political scene, and would be a defining feature of post-Independence Africa. In fact, since independence, there have been over 200 attempted coups in Africa, including successful ones in Zimbabwe in November 2017 and Sudan in 2019.[34]

Independence in North Africa came much sooner than it did for West, East, Central or Southern Africa. The first country south of the Sahara to gain its independence was Ghana (known as the Gold Coast under British rule), which did so in 1957 after a successful independence movement led by **Kwame Nkrumah**. At first Nkrumah seemed to be an enlightened leader intent on seeing democracy be successful in Ghana. However, Nkrumah incurred massive debts from his plans to build an electric power source using a dam on Lake Volta, the world's largest artificial lake. Yes, artificial—meaning man-made. Corruption and economic stagnation followed. He was overthrown in a coup in 1966, beginning a series of coups that wouldn't end until Jerry Rawlings, a political reformer, allowed the transition back to democracy by peacefully stepping aside when he was defeated after two terms in office in 2001.

In Kenya and Algeria, the presence of settlers and use of settler rule by the British and French made independence much more difficult to obtain. Many European settlers had lived in the colonies for much of their lives and were determined to stay. Equally as determined to gain their independence, Africans in both countries began armed uprisings against the settlers.

In Algeria, nationalists formed the National Liberation Front (French abbreviation FLN) that led to a **guerrilla war** in 1954. France was reeling from the loss of its Vietnamese colony, and deployed half a million troops to put down the rebellion. Atrocities on both sides terrified civilians. The Algerians turned to terrorism in the French parts of the city, and the French forces responded by authorizing torture of any suspected FLN rebels. A former French general in Algeria, Paul Aussaresses, wrote later that "torture...was tolerated if not recommended."[35]

Eventually public opinion in France turned so deeply against the war that the French government withdrew forces in 1962, but not after leaving behind a nation scarred by war and one that, like Egypt and Ghana, experienced its fair share of coups in the following years. A civil war between an Islamist party that won the elections in 1992 and the military raged for seven years and killed 100,000 people.[36] Still today, Algeria remains rife with tensions and accusations of fraudulent elections.

Year of Africa

The year 1960 was nick-named the **Year of Africa** because 17 countries gained their independence that year. The promise of independence was great-but the colonial legacy left behind would continue to create chaos in many countries for years to come.

In 1960 the Belgian Congo gained its independence. A man named **Patrice Lumumba** was elected the first Prime Minister, and with the massive country still reeling from decades of being a rubber plantation, appealed to the Soviet Union for help in putting down rebels in the province of Katanga.

The United States saw Lumumba's request as an attempt to ally himself (and his resource-rich country) with their communist nemesis, and secretly began supporting

Mobutu Sese Seko changed the name of the Belgian Congo to Zaire (now known as the Democratic Republic of Congo). Here he meets with the US Defense Secretary. Photo by Frank Hall, 1983.

his rival, Colonel **Mobutu Sese Seko**. With the assistance of the Central Intelligence Agency of the United States, Sese Seko captured and killed Lumumba, and began ruling as a military dictator in 1965.[37]

Mobutu was an unstable ruler. He viciously persecuted any suspected opponents and contributed to the poverty and corruption of the continually plagued Congo. Not until 1997 was he driven from power, but civil war over the bountiful resources of the Congo continues.

The example of the Congo perfectly illustrates a problem many African countries experienced: that of the resource curse. Though a country's wealth of natural resources should help it prosper, in this case, paradoxically, it has contributed to decades of war,

44

poverty, instability, and corruption.

The genocide that took place in neighboring Rwanda in 1994 also led to thousands of refugees and perpetrators of the conflict seeking a safe haven in the eastern part of the country. Some of the highest rates of disease, poverty, and violence in the world exist in this region of Eastern Congo due to its long history of conflict, beginning with King Leopold II.

Section Five Questions

1. Describe the pressures from outside of Africa as well as those from inside of Africa that contributed to the independence of many African countries. How does the Cold War, communism, and capitalism contribute to Africa's modern history?

2. What is the Year of Africa? Why do you think so many countries gained their independence then?

3. Why do you think coups have been so common since independence? What steps might need to be taken in order to bring more stability to these types of governments?

2.6 The Apartheid Era

One of the first African countries to gain its independence was South Africa, in 1910 ~ however, the independence was not for the black African population, but for a group of white Afrikaners, descendants of early Dutch settlers who had first landed in South Africa in 1652. The British, upon leaving South Africa, agreed to put the Afrikaners in charge, whom made up less than 20% of the country's population.[38] The black inhabitants were denied the right to vote, live where they desired, or even travel anywhere without white permission. These restrictions were known as the pass laws.

Apartheid sign from the District Six Museum.

Nelson Mandela in 2008. From The Good News, South Africa.

The strict classification of the races into White, Black, Coloured (mixed race) and Asian led to a severe separation of the races called **apartheid**. Afrikaner leaders insisted it was to help preserve the culture of each race, but in reality it was designed to consolidate and ensure complete White control over the entire country. Blacks were restricted to living in slums called townships and were sometimes forcibly relocated to these areas outside the main cities. Massive populations were forced to live in these townships, while the minority white population was allowed to live wherever they wished.

Resistance to these laws came in the form of the African National Congress (ANC), a group that fought against apartheid using protests, boycotts, and strikes to bring attention to the extreme discrimination in their country. One of the reasons that other countries, such as the United States, had not pressured the South African government to end apartheid was fear that a new, post-apartheid government could side with the Soviet Union, America's Cold War enemy. Once the Cold War ended, support for the ANC skyrocketed. By 1994, all black citizens were allowed to vote for president. South Africans overwhelmingly elected ANC leader Nelson Mandela, who had been imprisoned for 27 years in a jail cell on Robben Island for protesting the polices of apartheid. Though the end of apartheid was a tremendously positive change for South Africans, many Blacks are still concentrated in the **townships** like Langa.

A man walks down the street in a poorer section of the Langa township, a remnant of apartheid, in 2012.

Unemployment and poverty remain high among the Black community in South Africa.

The Resource Curse

Let's suppose that there is a super comfortable couch in the back of your classroom, and occasionally a student in the class asks your teacher if they can sit on the cushions during a film or presentation. Once this request is granted, however, what often happens is that there is a mad dash towards the couch. Limbs go flying, friends are shoved out of the way, and it is a full on battle for that last remaining cushion between three or four people that can really get ugly fast. When you look back at the couch, all you see is an old wooden frame strewn with papers, candy wrappers, and broken pencils. No one wants to sit on that couch now. What was once a blessing of resources is now a curse, and many of those students that didn't get a couch cushion are bruised and betrayed from the scuffle.

Certain countries in Africa have experienced a similar phenomenon, but on a much more serious and devastating level. Sierra Leone was blessed with an abundance of diamonds, which has helped fuel a civil war and the first documented use of child soldiers in the world. In the Democratic Republic of Congo, the resource curse began with Henry Stanley claiming it for King Leopold II, who set up rubber farms that enslaved the population and mutilated its workforce. Since independence, rubber has not been the only resource that has caused conflict between groups ~ one of the materials that make up your cell phone is widely mined in the Congo, which has set up an armed race for possession of these mineral-rich mines. The government in Congo borders on a state of anarchy, a country without a government, which has been worsened in recent years by an influx of refugees and fighters from the **Rwanda genocide** of 1994.

The Rwanda Genocide: A Lasting Legacy of Colonization

The original colonial power in Rwanda was Germany. Germany lost all of their African colonies after their defeat in World War I, and Belgium took control of Rwanda in 1918. When the Belgians arrived they categorized the people they found there into two main groups. The Belgians believed that the smaller group of people, who were herders, were taller and had thinner noses. They called these people the **Tutsis**, and put them in charge of the daily routines of the colony because to the Belgians, they looked more "European". The larger group of people were farmers, and to the Belgians, they appeared shorter and had wider noses. These people they called the **Hutus**. To further solidify these groups, they issued **ethnic identification cards**, which all Rwandans were required by law to carry.

Imagine if all the blondes in your class were designated to be the most capable of ruling the classroom, even though they were a minority of the students? How would they rule? How would you feel towards them?

Over time, many Hutus grew to resent the Tutsis, who received education and special treatment in the colony, despite being only about 15% of the population. The resentment reached a breaking point when, in 1962, the Belgians finally felt the crushing tide of independence upon their colony and agreed to leave. Before they did so, however, they attempted one last

The Ntrama Church Altar. Over 5,000 people seeking refuge were killed in this chapel. Photo taken by Scott Chacon, 2006.

time to save their stake in the land ~ they switched their favoritism from the Tutsis to the Hutus, putting the majority group in power, and hoping to gain the favor of the Hutus towards Belgian colonial rule.

It didn't work.

When the Hutus assumed control of the country, riots and attacks on Tutsis forced many to flee to neighboring countries. There they formed a rebel group called the **Rwanda Patriotic Force** or RPF, which was based in Uganda. Meanwhile, tensions between the groups continued to build until they reached a climax in 1994. The President of Rwanda, **Juvenal Habyarimana**, and the RPF reached a treaty in August of 1993 that would mean the two groups would share power in the country, and the United Nations sent an observer force of 2,500 troops to help set up the new government.

On April 6th, 1994, as the terms of the peace accords were about to be implemented, a plane carrying President Habyarimana and the President of neighboring Burundi was mysteriously shot down.

To this day, the group that shot down the plane is unknown.

However, many extremist Hutus in the country were looking for an excuse to launch a widespread and brutal attack on the Tutsis. One of these Hutu groups was called the **Interhamwe**, and they were a loosely organized militia that sought the destruction of all Tutsis and were directed by a radio station called RTLM Hutu Power Radio. When the plane was shot down, RTLM took to the radio waves and blamed the RPF for shooting down the plane (even though a peace agreement had been reached). RTLM directed the Interhamwe to begin attacking all Tutsis they could find, including women and children.

Skulls of some of the 800,000 people killed in 100 days of genocide in Rwanda. Taken in 2010 by configmanager at the Rwanda Genocide Memorial in Kigali, one of numerous memorials in the country.

What made their job much easier was the fact that one of the legacies of colonization in Rwanda was the ethnic ID cards that all Rwandans were legally required to carry. This identified potential victims for the Interhamwe and the Rwandan Armed Forces, who killed almost 1 million Tutsis in 100 days. [39]

The international community was horrified by the events in Rwanda, but had also been burned in another African country less than six months earlier.

The movie Black Hawk Down popularized the story of American Army Rangers undertaking a dangerous operation to remove a Somali warlord, **General Aideed**, who was controlling Somalia's capital city of Mogadishu. Two helicopters crashed in the mission, and several American soldiers were killed. A few of their bodies were even dragged through the streets, an event that was videotaped and broadcast to American homes. Many Americans were outraged at then-President Clinton for even having troops in Somalia and risking American lives in a conflict in which they had no stake in the outcome. This event was fresh in the mind of President Clinton when he decided to pull out all American peacekeepers and civilians from Rwanda during the genocide. Other countries followed suit and removed their peacekeepers. It was not until the RPF took back over the country and pushed the Interhamwe into the Democratic Republic of Congo that the genocide ended, 100 days later. Still today, unimaginable violence takes place in the northeastern corner of Congo, a region called Goma, where many of the murderers fled.

South Sudan Independence Day Celebration at Diversey Harbor Grove, Daniel X. O'Neil, 2011.

Darfur and the World's Newest Country

Sudan used to be Africa's largest country. Until 1956, it was ruled by the Egyptians in the North, and the British in the South. After independence, an Islamic government dominated the country from the northern capital of Khartoum, where Omar al-Bashir, a favorite villain of the West, ruled from 1989 until 2019, when he was overthrown in a coup.

The country is intensely diverse, with the North being predominantly Muslim and of Arab ethnicity, looking a lot like North Africa. In the South, many Sudanese are Christian or Animist, and are from many different Sub-Saharan tribes, such as the Dinka.

Many people in the North survive by herding cattle, while the majority of those in the South are farmers. These divisions came to a head in the northwestern region of the country called Darfur, where climate change and scarce water led to conflicts between Arab herders from the North, backed by the government, and tribal farmers from the South, many of whom wanted to separate from the North and its history of oppression and discrimination towards Southerners. This led to two prolonged periods of civil war, which ended with a peace agreement in 2005 that granted the South the right to secede - six years later. Thus, the brand-new country of **Southern Sudan** secured its independence in 2011.

Being the world's newest country isn't easy, especially when border disputes (many involving which country gets control of the South's oil reserves) continue to fuel tensions. In September 2012, the military of the country accidentally killed 10 of its own troops when it sank one of their riverboats that it believed was an enemy ship. Then it accidentally shot down a UN helicopter a few months later.

One Party Rule and the Death of Democracy

When the Year of Africa occurred in 1960, many people were hopeful that the transition to sovereignty or control over their own countries would lead to greater opportunities for all. The reality, however, has been that those who were educated and favored under colonial rule continued to have all of the economic, educational, and political opportunities in the country. This has led to a huge number of coup d'etats, or takeovers of the government, by groups that desire to enjoy the spoils of the ruling group.

The most basic definition of democracy is that people have the chance to vote for their leaders. However, in many African countries, there is only one political party to choose from! This scenario is called one-party rule. The upside to this system is that there are fewer disagreements since all candidates share the same political ideas and goals of the party. The downside is that those who don't share these ideas are left off of the ballot.

Africa Today

What does the future hold for this continent? There are many changes afoot. The first is that people are moving to the cities in massive numbers. Lagos, Nigeria, will soon overtake Cairo, Egypt, as Africa's largest city. The overall average age of the continent is quite young, as opposed to China, which is aging rapidly.

Politically, there are signs of real progress. From the immediate years following independence up until 1991, not a single African leader was voted out of office peacefully (unless you count the island of Mauritius). From 1991 until 2012, however, there have been 30 ruling parties or leaders that have left peacefully. Gradually, African political systems are changing from one-party to multi-party, even if many of those elections are still rigged.

The **Arab Spring**, a series of revolts against long-standing authoritarian rulers in North Africa and the Middle East, removed tyrants in Libya and Egypt and ignited smaller revolutions throughout the continent. Mauritania and Algeria remain under military rule, and although international organizations such as the United Nations spend millions of dollars a year to ensure free and fair elections, many countries, such as the Congo, Nigeria, and Rwanda, have suffered from accusations of wide-ranging election malpractices. Long-standing dictators from Zimbabwe and Sudan were overthrown in 2017 and 2019, respectively.

Economically, many nations of Africa are experiencing a surge in growth. China has taken notice and is investing heavily in mineral and oil-rich areas, such as Ghana and Nigeria.

Conflict continues to plague Sudan, Chad, the Central African Republic, Mali and Egypt. Many of these conflicts have roots in colonial rule, and peace in many cases will mean power-sharing agreements between ideologically opposed groups.

Section Six Questions

1. What is apartheid, who fought against it, and how are its effects still felt today?

2. Describe the Rwandan genocide and how Belgian rule contributed to it.

3. What is the resource curse? Create a fictional example of the resource curse in action.

CHAPTER 3: THE MIDDLE EAST

Women were an integral part of the success of the Tahrir Square protests in Egypt. President Mubarak eventually stepped down after 39 years in power. Photo credit Myriam Abdelaziz via oxfamnovib, 2011.

Perhaps no region we study this year is more controversial, more complex, or more fascinating than the Middle East. Let's start with this: it's not a continent - it's three continents: Europe, Asia, and Africa, all together. Experts argue about what constitutes the region of the Middle East and how many countries it has exactly. And while they've been arguing, the United States has fought three wars there since 1991. Osama bin Laden. Oil. Deserts (not desserts!). 9/11. Al-Qaeda. Camels. Aladdin. Misconceptions about the Middle East, based on these few broad stereotypes, can be as common as cat memes on the internet.

The wheel. The school. The alphabet. These inventions are so commonplace in our lives that it almost makes one's brain hurt to imagine a world without them (well, maybe not the school part). But in truth, humans got along okay without them. That is, until the arrival of the **Sumerian**s, one of the world's first true civilizations.

The Sumerians settled down and began farming between the Tigris and Euphrates rivers, an area the Greeks called **Mesopotamia**, in 3500 BCE (we call it Iraq, which is a bit shorter). This area lay within the **Fertile Crescent**, a curved region of highly fertile soil from the Eastern Mediterranean through Iraq down to the Persian Gulf where most of the world's first civilizations began.

Sumerian currency. Note the wedge-shaped cuneiform that marks the tablet. Photo credit Gavin Collins.

Like the Egyptians, the Sumerians settled in Mesopotamia because the mineral-rich soil along the riverbanks provided an ideal place for crops~and moving around all the time gets old fast! Once people started farming, cities began to grow, and there was time for people to specialize in jobs and have time to think about such fun and daunting questions as the meaning of life.

Religion flourished - the Sumerians were polytheistic, meaning they believed in many gods. They built temples called **ziggurats** (a great name for a band) that were much like the pyramids in Egypt~except these were tiered and off-limits to anyone who wasn't a priest. Also, you weren't allowed to put dead people in them.

The Sumerians had the time to create a system of wedge-shaped letters called **cuneiform**, and could send their children to schools where they might be able to learn such an elite skill as writing! The Sumerians and their inventions were eventually incorporated, along with the other city states of Mesopotamia, into a larger **Babylonian** empire around 1792

U.S. Soldiers tour the famous Ziggurat of Ur. Photo credit US Army.

BCE.[40] The Babylonians were led by a ruler named **Hammurabi**, who left a powerful legacy of his own.

Though his code of laws was not the world's first, it is the world's oldest surviving law code. His 282 laws, which we call **Hammurabi's Code**, were written in stone on pillars placed throughout his empire. One of these stone carvings is actually in the Louvre in Paris! Hammurabi's code was wide-ranging but paints the picture of a peaceful and well-run society, in which justice was a priority. There were laws that set a minimum wage, established a state-run economy, managed interest rates, inheritances, divorce and even alimony payments (in the Babylonian case, what a man must pay his ex-wife).

Hammurabi believed that the punishment should fit the crime. Today, because of our short attention spans, we refer to his code simply as "an eye for an eye", and in some cases, mutilation and death were fitting punishments for the most heinous of crimes. Overall though, Hammurabi is thought of by experts to be a ruler who cared greatly about peace and justice in his society. When Hammurabi died, the Babylonians fell victim to an invasion by the **Hittite**s. The law code was no match for the Hittites' invention of iron weapons, which allowed them to conquer all of Turkey and Mesopotamia.

Meanwhile, to the West of all this Mesopotamia action lay the civilization of the **Phoenicians** in Lebanon and Syria. They avoided being conquered for years because they were people of the sea who made their living through trade across the Mediterranean. Their sophisticated sails allowed them to travel long distances, even circumnavigating (going all the way around) Africa 2000 years before the Europeans did!

As the Phoenicians went from Lebanon to North Africa to Greece, they developed an alphabet of 22 characters that is the foundation of our alphabet today. These characters stood for consonants, and, like the language of Arabic today, readers would mentally add in the vowels as they read. When the Greeks adopted this script, they added the vowels, tweaking the alphabet into the basis of all Western alphabets today, including ours. Thanks, Phoenicians!

The Phoenician civilization, like their alphabet, was eventually incorporated into the Greek world when their capital city of Tyre was taken over by Alexander the Great in 322 BC. Again, these law code advancements and alphabets were no match for war.

The Persians

In the 6th century BCE (remember, that's 500 BCE), King Cyrus the Great established one of the world's largest empires in modern-day Iran. They called themselves the Irani, but the Greeks, noting their capital in the province of Persis, called them the **Persians**. As is often the case in history, outside of Persia the Greek name spread.

Cyrus the Great was a tolerant ruler who famously allowed 40,000 Jews to move back into Palestine in 537 BCE. Different cultures, traditions, and religions were tolerated during his rule. His successor, **Darius the Great**, extended the Persian empire all the way to India, and established a sophisticated road, tax and postal system. He implemented a system of coining money and even had spies that acted as the king's "eyes and ears." Under Darius, the royal city of Persepolis was built, which lends its name to the popular graphic novel and film adaptation about a teenage girl's life in Iran in the 1970's.

The Birth and Spread of the Abrahamic Religions

An illustration of (from left) Sarah, Hagar, Ishmael and Abraham. By Jim Padgett, Sweet Publishing, 1984.

Around 1700 BCE, according to the religions of Judaism, Christianity, and Islam, a man named **Abraham** was called to leave his successful life in Mesopotamia (Iraq) and move to the Promised Land of Canaan (in the modern-day country of Israel). Abraham lived in a society of polytheists, and his father made the idols, or figurines, that the people worshipped. Early in his life, Abraham smashed these figurines to prove to those around him that the idols themselves had no power.

Abraham's story is one of trials repeated throughout the Torah, Bible, and Quran. In each story, Abraham's faith is tested to an extreme degree, and because his faith never falters, Abraham is rewarded. Though called by God to expand monotheism through growing his family, he finds his wife, Sarah, is barren (unable to have a child). So Sarah convinces Abraham to try to bear a child by the maid, Hagar. This son, named Ishmael, will become the patriarch (father) of the Muslims. Thirteen years after Ishmael's birth, as a reward for Sarah's sacrifice, she too is granted a son, who is known as Isaac, patriarch of the Israelites.

The Torah, Bible, and Quran give different names and versions of each story. Religious scholars, historians, and anthropologists all debate about the existence of these people or whether they are composites (many different people) being used to tell a broader story. Whichever (if any) belief system you hold, it is important to know the fundamentals underlying these three huge monotheistic religions: that Abraham was the Father of Monotheism, that his faith was tested many times in many ways and always affirmed, and that his sons Ishmael and Isaac went on to lead new clans in new nations. The basic outline of this story informs millions of people's religious identities across the world. The differences, however, between all of these religions often continue to create conflict in our world today.

Judaism

Jews believe in Abraham as the messenger of God and in Moses as the man God entrusted with his laws. The Jewish Talmud and Torah are the two books Jews use to encode and decipher what laws should govern the community. The degree to which Jews follow these laws classifies them into secular, observant, or orthodox. Jews do not consider Jesus to be the son of God or for Muhammad to be a prophet.

Christianity

Christianity is an off-shoot of Judaism. It is important for you to remember that Judaism, Christianity, and Islam are all off-shoots of Abraham's first proclamation of monotheism ("There's just one god, you guys"). Throughout history there have been special allowances in each other's religions for these "People of the Book" as opposed

The holy Kaaba in Mecca, Saudi Arabia. Photo credit Turki Al-Fassam, 2008.

to other religions, like Hinduism and Buddhism, which do not share this tie.

In the Christian religion, there are three dimensions to God: the Father, the Son (Jesus Christ), and the Holy Spirit. Christian texts are based off of Jewish texts, but do not follow Jewish law. Christians consider Jewish law to be boiled down to "love thy neighbor as thyself." There is a history of tension between Christian and Jewish communities, particularly in Europe, where smaller minority sects of Judaism have often faced oppression. Christians have also bumped heads with the growth of Islam in the 1000s, leading to a wave of Crusades or military campaigns to stop the rising tide of the religion.

Islam

Islam began in 622 CE in Saudi Arabia and was founded by the Prophet **Muhammad**. It borrowed parts of the Jewish and Christian religions as well as from the nomadic tribes called the Bedouin, who lived in this area.

Around 570 CE, Muhammad was born in **Mecca**. He lost both of his parents at a young age and was raised by his uncle Abu Talib. Muhammad was a merchant with a reputation of trustworthiness, who at age 25 began working for a wealthy 40 year old widow named Khadija. She would become a very important contributor to the founding and growth of the religion, so you'll want to know her name. They were married and together they had six children, of which four daughters lived. After her death, Muhammad had nine wives - but bore children with none of them - and established these marriages mostly to create diplomatic bonds with other clans.

When Muhammad was 40 years old, he began hearing strange voices and having visions and sought solitude in a cave outside of Mecca on Mount Hira. After many days in the cave, the angel Gabriel appeared to Muhammad.

Terrified that he was being attacked by an evil spirit, Muhammad fled down the mountain, but the angel continued to speak to him, identifying itself as the angel Gabriel and Muhammad as God's one true messenger. There were further messages that encouraged Muhammad to spread this truth about one God (Mecca was mostly polytheistic at the time). These messages would make up the Quran, the holiest book in Islam.

So, even though he was reluctant at first, and even tried to jump off a mountain initially, Muhammad began to proclaim to his community that there was only one God. And boy, did he proclaim! But unfortunately, his proclamations were bad for business in Mecca. Muhammad encouraged social and economic justice, an end to female infanticide (killing female babies to ensure male offspring) and of course, an end to idol worship (which would put all of those idol makers out of business). Political and economic leaders within Mecca began to isolate Muhammad and his few followers, which were mostly young, lower and middle class folk.

Things really took a turn for the worse when Khadija and Muhammad's uncle, Abu Talib, passed away. Mecca's rulers then forced Muhammad out of Mecca in 622, forcing him on a pilgrimage that would take him north to a city known as Yathrib, where things finally began to turn around for Muhammad. As a result, the Muslim calendar officially begins in 622 (their year zero) so when calculating the year in the Muslim calendar for religious events, be sure to subtract 622 from the Gregorian calendar (what most countries around the world use as their official administrative calendar, and the one you are familiar with).

Once in Yathrib, Muhammad slowly began winning over converts to this religion. People who converted to Islam were bound by their belief in one god, rather than to their clan, which had been the case in Arabia for thousands of years. Thus, over the course of his ten years there, the city in which Islam grew became known as **Medina**, the "city of the prophet". Muhammad tried hard to win over the Jews and convert them to his religion, even encouraging worshippers to face towards Jerusalem for a time, as the Jews did. When his efforts were rebuked, followers returned to facing towards Mecca, as they do today.

Muhammad briefly returned to Mecca, having many more followers and now an army, which he unleashed on the city when one of his followers was killed, leading to the city's surrender. But he treated even the pagans well when ruling the city, prompting visitors from all over the region to visit this man who had conquered Arabia. Though he was now acknowledged as the leader of the city, he went back to live in Medina.

The religion grew, with the **Five Pillars of Islam** (charity, pilgrimage to Mecca called the Hajj, fasting during **Ramadan**, proclaiming the belief in one god, and prayer 5 times a day) guiding Muhammad's followers.

In 632 CE, at age 60, after a brief illness, Muhammad died, without designating who should succeed him in leading the growing group of Muslims in Arabia. This lack of a designated leader would lead to a deep division in the religion that remains to this day.

The Sunni/Shia Split and Sufism

When Muhammad died it was a pivotal point for Muslims. Here they were, with a religion in its infancy, gaining followers and political power, but with their most charismatic leader deceased! What to do?

Some Muslims argued that the next leader of Islam should be a relative of the prophet, and chose **Ali**, Abu Talib's son and Muhammad's cousin. These Muslims became known as the party of Ali or Shia'at Ali - today known as the **Shia** or Shiites. They are the smaller sect of Islam, with majorities in Iran, Lebanon, and Bahrain, and significant minorities in Iraq and Syria.

Other Muslims believed that the "best" Muslim, meaning the most righteous and pious as decided by the people, should lead them. These people became known as the **Sunnis**, and make up the majority of Muslims around the world - between 87%-90% according to most recent estimates.[41]

Sufis are a third and much smaller branch - they represent more mystical interpretations of Islam. The most distinctive feature of Sufism is its method of prayer - a whirling dance with a big open skirt that is mesmerizing - those who are chosen to become "whirling dervishes" must go through years of training to master this difficult and highly sacred practice.

Unfortunately, the split between Sunnis and Shiites was a violent one. Ali, and then his two sons, were both killed in conflicts between the two groups over who should be the one true caliph, or leaders of the Muslims. As a result, the Shia adopted rituals of grieving and martyrdom that are very different than those the Sunni have.

Section One Questions

1. Explain how Islam, Christianity and Judaism are similar and how Islam split into two different sects. You can use diagrams, but your explanation should fill at least a half page and explore each issue deeply.

2. Give three examples of religious similarity and three examples of religious difference you witness in our world today - that's six total examples.

3.2 The Middle East Comes West

Two very successful dynasties of Islam, that of the Umayyad and the Abbasid family, expanded the religion to Africa, Europe, and deeper into Asia. The Umayyads came first and discriminated against other cultures while promoting Muslim arts and scholarship, whereas the Abbasids embraced other cultures and saw an era of peace and innovations.

By the 11th century, the Christian powers in Europe were worried about the growing influence of Islam in the holy land in particular. A new dynasty, the Seljuk Turks, had taken control of what is known today as Israel and was re-

Crusaders attack Constantinople in this illustration, circa 1330. This drawing is from an early 14th-century edition of the knight and crusader Geoffrey of Villehardouin's account of the attack.

stricting Christian pilgrims from accessing it. Alarmed, **Pope Urban II** rallied Christian armies to fight back and reclaim the holy land for the Christians.

The First of the Crusades

In 1096, a desperate call was issued. The group that responded was made up mostly of peasants from Germany and France. They made their way across Europe, generally causing quite a lot of damage, but were defeated when they got to modern-day Turkey.

The next crusade was a bit more organized. It was made up of knights instead of peasants, and reached Jerusalem in 1099. They took over the prized holy land and controlled it for almost fifty years. Muslim armies eventually recaptured one of the other Christian-controlled states in the Middle East (so-called "Crusader states") in 1144. Again, the call went out for Christian fighters to recapture the holy lands in the Middle East. Again, its armies were decimated crossing from Europe into the Middle East.

During the Third Crusade, historians found their leading men. **Saladin**, the leader of the Turks, is widely believed to be one of the greatest Muslim commanders of all time. Saladin captured Jerusalem, beginning the third wave of Christian crusaders charging from Europe to the Middle East. The most famous Christian commander of the Crusades, Richard I or **Richard the Lionheart**, led the effort ~ but ultimately failed in his goal of controlling Jerusalem. However, Richard the Lionheart and Saladin were able to reach an agreement by which Christians could have access to the Holy City.

Another misadventure of particular note was the disastrous Children's Crusade of 1212. Part legend and part fact, this period of religious zeal was led by two tweens: Stephen (12) of France and Nicholas (10) of Germany. Miraculously, these pint-size believers amassed an army of thousands to retake Jerusalem. Unfortunately, instead of getting onto a ship bound for Jerusalem, some of Nicholas's group ended up on a boat destined for Alexandria, where they were sold into slavery. [42]

This map depicts the Ottoman Empire's extent in 1683. By the end of WWI in 1918, Turkey is all that is left. Atilim Gunes Baydin, based on Robert Mantran, Histoire de l'Empire Ottoman.

Five Crusades later, the Christians lost their last stronghold in the area in 1291. The Muslims reoccupied Jerusalem, and the era of the Crusades was over.

The Ottoman Empire

In the late 13th century, a group of Turkish Muslims united to combat the shrinking Christian Byzantine empire. This group gained followers, and in 1453, they took over the Byzantine capital of Constantinople in modern-day Turkey, which was later renamed Istanbul. Under Suleiman the Magnificent in the 16th century, the Ottomans reached their height, controlling most of the Middle East, and much of North Africa and Southeastern Europe.

The Ottoman Empire was ruled by sultans, who acted as the political and religious rulers of the land. They delegated many of their day-to-day duties to pashas, or governors, of their many provinces. This centralized government worked for the first part of Suleiman's rule, but near the end of his reign the sultans became weak and the pashas began combating rebellions from local groups.

The end of the empire came after World War I, in which the sultan sided with the Central Powers of Germany and Austria-Hungary in their fight against the Allied Powers of Britain, America, Russia, France, and Serbia (what I affectionately refer to as the BARFS). After the revolts from Arab groups led by British military hero **Lawrence of Arabia**, the Ottomans signed the **Treaty of the Sevres** in 1917, ending their involvement. This Treaty gave Britain and France the former Ottoman provinces of Syria, Lebanon, Iraq, Jordan, Palestine (modern-day Israel) and Kuwait.

And here is where you really have to pay attention. Because so many of the problems in the Middle East today come down to this fateful split of territory in 1917, it is important to analyze what forces were at work in the split, and what the outcomes were.

There are many times in history when treaties have led to fundamentally massive shifts in territory, culture and rule and this is one of them. Can you think of two from our previous studies?

Let's start with Israel and Palestine, what has been a contentious strip of land since it was proclaimed the "Promised Land" by the Israelites and occupied by Moses and the Hebrews around 1000 BC.

This same strip of land was conquered by the Greeks and Romans who called the people they encountered there the "Philistines," which translated roughly to the modern-day Palestinians.

Then Jesus Christ was born, practiced, and died in the same land ~ making his route sacred to future generations of Christians.

But wait, there's more! The Muslims conquered the same land around 640 and had their own religious experience to cite when Muhammed briefly stopped at the Dome of the Rock in Jerusalem before ascending to heaven. Outside of Saudi Arabia, the Dome of the Rock is the holiest site in all of Islam.

Three religions. One scrappy piece of turf. It's about to get interesting.

The Ottoman Turks, as we stated earlier, had control of this territory from the 1500s to the 1900s before the final death blow of WWII stripped the last remaining Middle Eastern territories from them. The crown jewel of course was Palestine, a land of enormous religious and also political significance.

At the same time, a small but determined group of European Jews calling themselves **Zionists** had begun a persistent campaign to convince the British of their birthright to the "Promised Land" of Israel, as was given to them by God in accordance with the Jewish religion. The British Foreign Secretary, **Alfred Balfour**, issued a declaration later called the **Balfour Declaration** that allowed small groups of European Jews to move into Palestine as World War I was breaking out, with the clear idea that there should be an independent state for Arabs and that the Jews should not interfere with the affairs of the current inhabitants.

On the sidelines, however, the British were also trying to woo the Arabs of the Middle East to join their cause. They sent in a handsome, charismatic, and ultimately very dedicated man named **Colonel T.E. Lawrence** to convince small Arab militias to fight back against the Ottoman Empire and thus rule their own lands for themselves.

These Arab armies, convinced by Lawrence "of Arabia" that the British intentions were to help them get their land from the Ottomans, were an effective fighting force and reason why the Ottoman Empire eventually had to pull out of World War I and sacrifice much of its territory to Britain and France. But...

Sneakily ~ the British and French had already made an agreement that assumed this outcome. Called the **Sykes-Picot Agreement**, this secret pact divided the spoils of the Ottoman Empire between themselves, leaving very little in the hands of the Arab militias that had been promised autonomy. The newly created territories of Syria and Lebanon went to the French, while the British claimed Iraq, Jordan, Palestine and Kuwait.

The Balfour Declaration and Sykes-Picot Agreement Aftermath

Predictably, when much of the Middle East fell into the control of the British and French, a sense of betrayal stirred many inhabitants. Further disputes began almost immediately between the Palestinians and the newly arrived Zionists. With the rise of Germany's Nazi Party in the 1930's, more and more Jewish settlers arrived in Palestine, convinced that this may be their only refuge from the targeted violence of Europe. After all, this was not the first time Jews had been singled out for horrific mistreatment.

Think back to our Russia unit, where one of the main targets of ethnic attacks had been the Jews, rounded up and often killed in what were called pogroms that were prevalent in Imperial Russia and into Stalin's reign. There were many reasons for Jews to fear ethnic attacks, which is one reason many families left everything they had back home in search of a promise of safety and security in Palestine.

Unfortunately, the safety and security of Palestine had been but a dream. Fighting continued from the Balfour Declaration all the way up to 1947, when the newly created United Nations (it was barely a toddler of 2 years old!) attempted to pass **Resolution 181**, hoping to appease both sides. Resolution 181 would have given 55% of the land to the Jews and 45% of the land to the Palestinians. Jerusalem would become an international city. A year later, a **War of Independence** (as the Jewish population calls it) or the **Naqba** (as the Palestinians call it, meaning catastrophe) broke out when Israeli Prime Minister David Ben-Gurion declared Israel an independent state on May 14, 1948.

The surrounding Arab countries of Syria, Transjordan, Lebanon, Iraq, and Egypt attacked the next day leading to the Arab-Israeli War of 1948.

An eight month long war ensued in which Israel made gains in the North and the South. The fate of over 700,000 Palestinian refugees now hung in the balance.[43] They scraped by in camps set up by the United Nations in the Gaza Strip (bordering Egypt) and West Bank (bordering Jordan), and those who could often fled the country, hoping to return some day.

Less than seven years later, in 1956, Israel became suspicious of arms deals that were going on between Egypt and the USSR. The Israeli military launched a preemptive attack on Egypt, occupying the Gaza Strip and Sinai Peninsula, which had been under Egypt's control. It took months for Israel to withdraw from the **Arab-Israeli Conflict of 1956**, and a UN Peacekeeping force was set up on the tense border to prevent future standoffs.

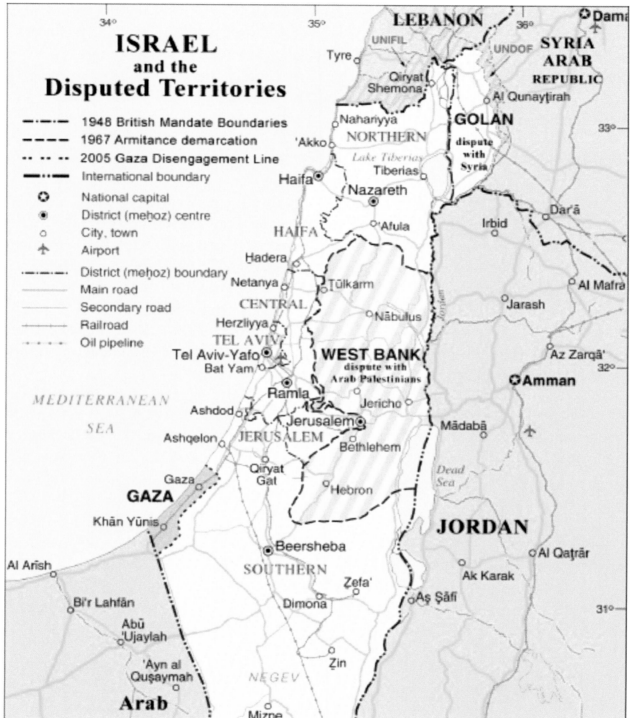

This map should give you a good idea of the size of the Gaza Strip and West Bank and the location of major conflict zones. Be sure to find Jerusalem, and observe why its location and significance to all three religions may make it a constant subject of dispute. "Israel and the Disputed Territories map" by Jaakobou modified from http://www.un.org/Depts/Cartographic/map/profile/israel.pdf via Wikimedia Commons.

Another Israeli preemptive strike was launched in 1967 during the **Six Day War**, in which Israel became suspicious of an Egyptian, Syrian, and Jordanian arms build-up near its border. Egypt's lone air force of 350 planes was destroyed on the ground, and 200 Arab tanks were annihilated in the short time of the conflict.[44] As a result, the territories of Gaza and the West Bank became permanently under the occupation of the **Israeli Defense Force** (IDF).

Further conflicts, such as a surprise attack by Arab forces against the Israeli Defense Force on Yom Kippur, the holiest day of the Jewish calendar, in 1973, temporarily called into question how invincibile the IDF, with the support of many Western European countries and the United States, could be. However, despite terrorist attacks and two prolonged periods of uprising called the **intifada**, Israeli territory continued to grow, while Palestinian territory continued to shrink. Enclaves built for Israeli settlers inside Palestinian territory cause tension, as do frequent checkpoints which make travel arduous if not impossible between Palestinian towns. Several rounds of peace talks, many mediated by US Presidents, have failed to address the main issues, which are: control of Jerusalem, the Right of Return for Palestinians who lost homes in 1947, guarantees from the Palestinians to renounce terror tactics, and an end to settlement building in Palestinian territories.

On very few of these issues has there been any real movement, despite much hope after the **Camp David Accords** (1978, in which Egypt acknowledged Israel's right to exist) and **Oslo Accords** (1993, in which the ruling authority of the Palestinians, called the PLO, and Israel acknowledged each other's right to exist, but led to the assassination of one of the key players of the peace movement, **Prime Minister Yitzhak Rabin**).

Today the conflict is at a standstill. Settlements continue to be built in the occupied territories. The refugee camps in Jordan, the West Bank, and Gaza continue to expand. Tensions simmer and then boil, as they did between Gaza and southern Israel in the fall of 2012 and the summer of 2014, when Israel once again demonstrated that its superior firepower and missile defense systems are largely unfazed by the poorly constructed rockets of militants in Gaza.

In 2018, President Trump announced that the US would move its embassy to Jerusalem. This prompted protests by Palestinians who claim that the US can no longer be a fair mediator in the peace process with the decision to recognize Jerusalem as the capital of Israel.

Section Two Questions

1. Explain in five steps how the current Israel-Palestine land conflict came to be. Be sure to include the Balfour Declaration and Six Day War.

2. What do you think the lasting outcome of the Sykes-Picot Agreement is?

3. Consider the Crusades. In what other scenarios have small rebel groups weakened a great empire?

4. Write out a fictional or real scenario in which the Balfour Declaration is happening with two groups of people today. One group is persecuted and seeking a safe home, and the other is caught off guard by the influx of new immigrants. Explain the conflict in one paragraph and your imagined resolution (can be peaceful or confrontational) in the second paragraph.

3.3 The Iran Hostage Crisis

For a number of reasons, Iran is a country we are going to take some time to focus on in this unit. Previously known as Persia (from the Persian empire you read about a few pages ago), this predominantly (mostly) Shiite country is regularly in the news a and will likely continue to be all throughout our study of the Middle East. Most of the coverage will focus on how the United States and Iran have a very contentious (tense) relationship and in the next few pages, we'll be examining why exactly that is.

Oil!

Oil was struck in 1908, by a company that is today known as British Petroleum (BP, you may have heard of them). This discovery, and the maneuvering of the British to get control of the oil fields of Iran, led to a lasting relationship between the rulers of Iran and the West.

"The Shah of Iran and President Nixon" by Robert Knudsen, National Archives and Records Service, 1969.

Reza Shah Pahlavi, known as the "Shah" or king in Iran, was installed on the throne from the time of WWII. He was big on modernizing and westernizing the country, and also was very close with Western interests, allowing much of the profits of the oil fields to flow out of the country. This angered many Iranians and the Shah began to lose his influence. Meanwhile the Prime Minister, Mohammad Mossadeq, gained favor with the people by nationalizing the foreign-dominated oil-industry in 1951.

The British immediately placed an oil embargo on Iran and began planning, with the American intelligence services, to overthrow Mossadeq. President Eisenhower approved a CIA-led mission to put the Shah firmly back into power in 1953.[45] This proved very unpopular.

To quash any dissent, the Shah created a secret police called the **SAVAK** (trained by the CIA) that brutally repressed any dissent in the country. One of the loudest and most popular voices speaking against the Shah was **Ayatollah Khomeini**, who the Shah had exiled.

Ayatollah Khomeini, 1972, Author unknown.

On New Year's Eve, 1977, President Jimmy Carter, visiting Iran, clinked glasses with the Shah, calling him "an island of stability" in the Middle East. The irony of this statement will soon be revealed.

Protests began brewing that same year. By January 16th, 1979, demonstrations in the streets grew to a fever pitch and protesters saw their opportunity. The Shah fled to Egypt and the Ayatollah returned to Iran after 14 years of exile.

By October, the Shah was pleading with the United States to allow him entry so he could receive medical treatment for his cancer. Meanwhile, the Ayatollah had declared Iran an Islamic Republic and demanded that the Shah face trial for the crimes committed by the SAVAK. When President Carter decided to allow the Shah entry into the U.S., Iranian college students directed their rage towards the United States embassy, demanding the Shah's return.

Without much protection, the embassy was overrun and 66 members of the staff were taken hostage (after 7 days, the Ayatollah ordered the release of black and female hostages because they already "felt the oppression of American society").

President Carter felt he had few options. Yellow ribbons marked solidarity with the hostages. Anchors counted the days on the nightly news report. Pressure was mounting by April 1980 for him to do something other than put an **embargo** (ban) on Iranian oil.

So he did. Have you ever heard of Delta Force? They were a top secret elite section of the air force that had just been created when President Carter decided to put them to use in the crisis. The plan, code-named Operation Eagle Claw, was for eight helicopters to land on the embassy roof and rescue the hostages.

Unfortunately, the brand new helicopters and pilots were not used to the desert conditions they faced. When only six helicopters reached the staging zone, the mission was aborted. As the force prepared to leave, one of the helicopters crashed into a transport plane, killing eight servicemen. It was a huge embarrassment for the Carter administration and may be one of the reasons he did not win re-election in 1980.

For 444 days, 52 hostages were kept in the embassy. Not until President Carter stepped down from office and President Reagan was inaugurated was their release secured.

The hostages return to America. Photo by Don Koralewski, 1980.

The Aftermath of the Crisis

Our relations with Iran since the **Islamic Revolution of 1979** and the Hostage Crisis have been quite frosty. While Iran has declared numerous times that they are not enriching uranium to create nuclear weapons, but only for nuclear power, the US remains skeptical and on alert, given our history.

In June of 2013, Iranians elected **President Rouhani**, a more moderate politician than the fiery Mahmoud Ahmadenijad that they endured for eight years, a man who denied the Holocaust and made numerous threats against the United States. Rouhani has shown some willingness to open up a dialogue with the West. Meanwhile, the United States' attention has shifted to more imminent threats all while keeping one cautious eye on Iran.

In 2015, the five members of the UN Security Council plus Germany (known as the P5+1) signed an historic agreement with Iran to reduce their nuclear capabilities. In exchange for more surveillance of Iran's nuclear facilities, the P5+1 loosened the strict restrictions on trade, called **sanctions**, allowing Iran to export oil once again. When Donald Trump was elected President of the United States in November of 2016, he indicated he might change the deal. He reimposed sanctions in May of 2018, prompting Iran to sue the United States in the International Court of Justice in July 2018. [46]

Section Three Questions

1. Explain why the Iranian Hostage Crisis began.

2. What plans were put in place to end the crisis?

3. How does the Hostage Crisis affect America's relationship with Iran today? What other conflict or situation from our earlier studies can you compare this relationship to?

4. Why might the United States want to prevent Iran from gaining a nuclear weapon? Why might Iran want to secure a nuclear weapon? Is it reasonable for the United Nations to try to limit the spreading of nuclear weapons to more countries? Why or why not?

3.4 The Persian Gulf War

In 1914, the Ottoman Empire joined Germany and Austria-Hungary in their war against France, Britain, Russia and the United States. When these Allied powers won, the Ottoman Empire was divided among Britain and France. Today's country of Turkey was all that was left for the Turks.

The British claimed Kuwait, Iraq, and Saudi Arabia. A British officer named **Sir Percy Cox** established these modern-day borders and put leaders in charge that he thought would be loyal and support their interests.

Saudi Arabia and Kuwait, though not entirely pleased, accepted these new borders. Iraq's leaders did not. They received a very small amount of coastline on the Persian Gulf, necessary for trading and a port. In addition, Iraq was created by cobbling together three former Ottoman provinces (Baghdad, Mosul, and Basra) with three completely different religious and ethnic groups with histories of tension. Their third argument with the new borders was that the new country of Kuwait, with a long and desirable coastline, had once been part of Ottoman Basra, and should be a part of Iraq. Following independence from Britain in 1932, Iraq's leaders would work tirelessly to re-acquire Kuwait for themselves.

In 1963 the **Ba'ath** Party overthrew the ruling government of Iraq. This political party was founded in the 1940s with the goal of reuniting the Arab world and making it one powerful nation ~ hopefully this reminds you of the concept of Pan-Africanism, and indeed, this idea is called **Pan-Arabism**.

After receiving a massive payment from the Kuwaiti government, Iraq finally recognized Kuwait's independence formally in 1963. But there continued to be a dispute over the Rumaylah oil field that lay between the two countries.

In August 1990, with a Ba'ath Party ruler named **Saddam Hussein** in charge, Iraq invaded Kuwait. Hussein was ruling a country deeply in debt from a bloody eight year war with neighboring Iran. Hussein figured he could make up some of that debt by gaining control of Kuwait's oil fields. If he suceeded, he could eliminate some of the millions of dollars in debt it owed to Arab nations ~ including $16 million to Kuwait.[47] What Hussein did not count on was that tiny Kuwait had a big ally with a major interest in keeping the country out of Iraq's hands.

"The liberation of Kuwait has begun."

The United States was an ally of Kuwait, but even more significantly, it was an ally of Saudi Arabia, its largest oil supplier. With Iraq fully in control of Kuwait, Saudi Arabia began to fear that it may be Hussein's next target. The United States, with a coalition of other forces from the United Nations, set up a protective military border between Saudi Arabia and Iraq in a mission called **"Operation Desert Shield"**.

U.S. Marines in the Persian Gulf War. Staff Sgt. Vance, 1991.

Then President George H.W. Bush (the elder Bush) gave Saddam Hussein an **ultimatum** ~ leave Kuwait by January 15, 1991, or risk a ground and air operation by the United States. But Hussein didn't blink.

On January 16, the US turned Operation Desert Shield into **Operation Desert Storm** - a campaign of air bombardment against the Iraqi military in Kuwait. The air campaign then morphed into a ground campaign titled - you guessed it - **Operation Desert Saber**. Within a few months, Iraq was in retreat and Kuwait had been liberated. Hussein, furious at the United States and even more deeply in debt, retreated to Baghdad. The United States did not pursue him into the country.

A very small group of extremists within Saudi Arabia were furious that "infidels" from America had set up military operations in the holy land during the military campaigns.

75

They would use this grievance as a reason to attack America ten years later, on September 11, 2001. Their leader, **Osama bin Laden**, would make it an important part of the anger that fueled the growth of his new terrorist group - **al-Qaeda**.

9/11, Al-Qaeda, Afghanistan: Aftermath of the Persian Gulf War

Al-Qaeda was formed in the 1990's by a wealthy relative of the Saudi royal family ~ a man named Osama bin Laden. Al-Qaeda, which means "the base" in Arabic, claims to be an Islamic terrorist organization, and has small groups or "cells" all over the world.

United Airlines Flight 175 hits the World Trade Center's South tower on 9/11. Photo by TheMachineStops.

When al-Qaeda members crashed their planes into the Pentagon, the Twin Towers, and a field in Pennsylvania with four planes on September 11, 2001, most people in America had never heard of the group or of Osama bin Laden. But quickly, and tragically, they were made aware.

If you ask someone close to you who is at least in their 30s, they will likely be able to remember exactly where they were when they heard about the attacks. Similarly, some of your elder relatives likely can tell you exactly where they were when we were attacked on December 7th, 1941 by the Japanese at Pearl Harbor or how they felt when they heard President John F. Kennedy had been shot. Certain events in our history just stay with us in a very visceral way. This is one of them for many people in your life and your community.

The government of the United States knew they needed to take action. Al-Qaeda was known to have a base in Afghanistan, where they were protected by an Islamic fundamentalist group that was in control of the country, called the Taliban. The Taliban are known for being extremely strict, particularly in the area of women's rights. Women must be covered head to toe in a burqa, may not leave the house unescorted by a male relative, may not work and may not attend school. In many cases, music, dancing, and alcohol are forbidden. Harsh punishments are dealt out to people who break these rules.

The Taliban, frustratingly enough, are an off-shoot of a group called the **Mujahideen**. The Mujahideen were a group of fighters who the American government secretly armed and funded in their fight against the Soviet Union during the Cold War. Some of them still use the military training and weapons given to them by America in the 1970s and 1980s during this war.

The Taliban has sheltered al-Qaeda for years. The United States decided to invade Afghanistan and go after al-Qaeda and Osama bin Laden. The military captured many top officials in both the Taliban and al-Qaeda, and set up a government in the capital of Kabul, with elections and democratic institutions. Unfortunately, Afghanistan is a spread out, mountainous, and very rural country ~ and so it was hard to keep the Taliban out for long. Meanwhile, many top leaders from al-Qaeda had already fled to the rugged border areas between Afghanistan and Pakistan. Osama bin Laden was discovered living in northern Pakistan in 2011 and killed by US Navy Seals. In 2020, President Trump made an agreement with the Taliban to withdraw American troops. As of July, the US maintains 8,600 American troops in the country, with 4,000 more expected to return to the US in the fall.

Meanwhile...in Iraq

Saddam Hussein appearing in an Iraqi courtroom in 2004. Photo by SSGT D. Myles Cullen.

Following the terrorist attacks of 9/11, America was on edge. With bin Laden still on the loose and the increasing fear of terrorism, President George W. Bush began to suspect Iraq was a potential host for terrorists. Declaring that Hussein had **Weapons of Mass Destruction** and had an "operational relationship" with al-Qaeda, the Bush administration pushed for an invasion of Iraq.

Though by all accounts Saddam Hussein was a harsh, oppressive, and murderous dictator, the allegations that there was any relationship between al-Qaeda and Iraq were disproved by the Joint Forces Command of the US military in 2008. In addition, in 2008, the CIA admitted there was no evidence that there ever were Weapons of Mass Destruction in Iraq.

Regardless, in March 2003, America went to war against Iraq. In December of 2003, Saddam Hussein was found hiding in an underground bunker. He was convicted of crimes against humanity and hung in 2006. It was not until December of 2011 that the US removed its final combat troops. In total, according to some estimates, nearly 5,000 U.S. troops were killed and over 500,000 Iraqis died.[48] Still today, car bombings and government corruption dominate the news on Iraq. Conflicts between the three different provinces continue to this day.

The Arab Spring

Mohammed Bouazizi did not set out to be a revolutionary.

He was a humble vegetable seller in Tunisia. Unable to afford college, he tried to survive by peddling vegetables to passers by. But he could not afford the required permit.

On December 17, 2011, a policewoman caught him. When he could not pay the fine, his family claimed that she slapped him and confiscated his cart. When he went to the local government to complain, they refused to see him. Then, in front of the building, frustrated and hopeless, he set himself on fire.

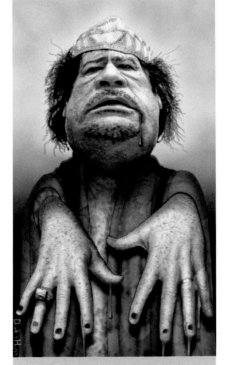

Dictator Muammar Qaddafi as a zombie. Drawn by artist DonkeyHotey, 2011.

This act awakened much of the long-simmering anger that had been brewing in Tunisia and across the Middle East. Anger about the lack of

Protesters march in support of vegetable seller Mohammed Bouazizi, whose actions triggered the Arab Spring. Photo by Antoine Walter, 15 January 2011.

opportunities, corruption, poverty, and greed in the government resulted in protests in the streets. Reaction to the protests that began in Tunisia were brutal and swift. But the protesters were unfazed. They continued, attracting attention around the world. Bouazizi died in the hospital from his injuries on January 4, but the protesters marched on. Ben Ali, a dictator who had ruled the country for 23 years, fled only 10 days later. His wife followed, taking much of the gold from the Central Bank with her.

Seeing the success in Tunisia, protesters in Egypt began to flood **Tahrir Square**, calling for the removal of their dictator of 30 years, **Hosni Mubarak**. They too were success-ful, in February of 2011.

Libya was next. Muammar **Gaddafi**, a wildly unstable ruler who traveled the world with an entourage of over 300 people and maintained an army of elite female bodyguards, was confronted with protesters.[49] His reaction was brutal and resulted in a civil war be-tween his regime and the people of Libya. The United Nations stepped in to create a no-fly zone and NATO began bombing Libyan military targets due to Gaddafi's bombing of civilian targets. In October of 2011, Gaddafi was pulled out of a sewer pipe where he was hiding and killed by rebels in the city of Sirte, the last remaining stronghold in the country.

Yemen and Syria followed suit. Syria's regime, led by President **Bashar al-Assad**, began killing protesters in the city of Deraa in March of 2011. Protests morphed into a civil war which continues to this day.

Yemen's uprising succeeded in removing their dictator of 33 years, Ali Abdullah Saleh, in 2012. The ensuing chaos led to a civil war in 2015 that is ongoing. Saleh was later assassinated in 2017.

Most of these uprisings have not solved the underlying problems. Egypt threw out its democratically elected president, **Mohammed Morsi**, after one year. It is now led by General-turned-President Abdel Fattah el-Sisi, who led the military coup to expel Morsi after seven months in 2013.

Syria's dictator Bashar al-Assad, in three pictures above in a window in Syria. James Gordon, 2006.

Libya is struggling to control the terrorist cells inside its country and recover from the crippling civil war which halted its oil industry, the main source of income for the country. Its prime minister was briefly abducted in October 2013 by the militias that were formed under Gaddafi's rule. Tunisia is struggling to protect members of its political minorities after a wave of assassinations.

Professor Noah Feldman of Harvard University, who aided Tunisians in writing their new Constitution, recently published a book called *Arab Winter: A Tragedy* in which he argues that "the Arab Spring ultimately made many people's lives worse than before." While not all historians and scholars go this far, the lack of progress in many Middle Eastern countries following these uprisings is a cause for concern.

Section Four Questions

1. Who is Saddam Hussein and what was his history with the United States?

2. What were the lasting effects of the Persian Gulf War on the region and on the United States?

3. Compare and contrast the Persian Gulf War with the Iranian Hostage Crisis.

4. What is the link between the Cold War and the Taliban?

5. Why did the United States go to war against Iraq in 2003? How long did the war last?

6. What are the causes and outcomes of the Arab Spring?

CHAPTER 4: LATIN AMERICA

"Colourful Cops in Mexico City" by Geraint Rowland, 2012, via Flickr Creative Commons.

Our next unit of study focuses on another region tied together by common languages, specifically the languages of Spanish and Portuguese, which both have a basis in - what else - Latin! Mexico, Central America, South America, and the Caribbean are our next area of focus and will involve potatoes, tomatoes, guns, horses, diseases, cigars, assassination attempts and all kinds of other fascinating historical anecdotes. Simon Bolivar, a famous liberator in Latin America, once said "America is ungovernable for us. He who serves a revolution plows the sea."

4.1 The Beginning

Did you know that the Ice Age is not just a collection of hilarious animated films? Of course you did. But the point is, it changed not just the lives of a few prehistoric mammals, but the migration patterns of millions!

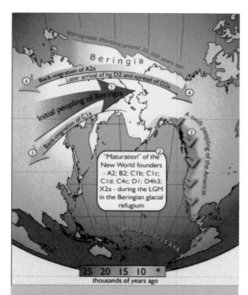

Map of the gene flow in and out of Beringia. Erika Tamm et al, 2007.

"A long time ago" - we're talking 50,000 years here, people - the world experienced a period of time so cold that the glaciers grew enormously in size, converting millions of gallons of sea water into tall glaciers and sucking that sea water out of the ocean. Ocean levels dropped, revealing, for the first time, a land bridge between Russia and Alaska called the Bering Land Bridge (because it is now covered with water, it is called the Bering Strait).

For decades, the most prevalent theory was that humans were tracking large game herds that migrated from Siberia across the land bridge to Alaska, and humans (who were hunting and gathering at the time) followed them. This theory is widely supported by most textbooks, but the first person to come up with it lived during the 1500s. More recently, some scholars have suggested that perhaps the first humans came not by foot but by boat, traveling down the "Kelp Highway" of the Pacific Coast. Human remains found earlier than the land bridge would have been passable by humans support this theory.

For a long time, humans continued to hunt and gather. But around 3000 BCE, in the area of Mexico, people began to settle down and begin farming. Corn, squash, and beans were the main sources of food for these early farmers, and continue to be major staples of many Latin American diets today.

The MAI: Latin America's First Great Civilizations

The **Maya** were the first "great" civilization to appear (and then, MYSTERIOUSLY disappear) in Latin America. Between 600 and 300 BCE (remember that we count down on the BCEs) the Mayan civilization was flourishing in the area around Guatemala. They had sophisticated systems of writing, trade, and paper-making, as well as a calendar of 365 and 1/4 days, created by the priests observations of the sky and diligent record-keeping.

Mayan Compass. Copyright Rik Friday, "Egyptian iBook of the Dead."

Many people believed (FALSELY) that the Mayans predicted that the end of the world would occur in December 2012 because their long-form calendar, which lasts 2,500 years, ended on December 21, 2012. What many people failed to realize, however, is that the Mayans believed a new long-form calendar would begin on December 22, 2012.[50] But that sort of historical footnote does not make a good Blockbuster film or sell t-shirts and key-chains.

Historical footnotes are important!

The Mayans had no central leader and no capital, but rather a sophisticated system of city-states. They believed strongly in gods that controlled the weather, crops, and fertility, among many other things. Often they would play a game called pok-a-tok, sort of like basketball but infinitely harder. You had to hit a 5 pound ball using your hips and forearms into a basket at the other end of the court. The losers were sometimes killed, and injuries were frequent. There were many religious beliefs surrounding the game, particularly that the sun would cease shining if they didn't continue playing the game.

Now Fitness class doesn't sound so bad, does it?

Historians aren't quite sure what caused the decline of the Mayan civilization around 300 CE. Theories include a famine, flood, invasion, or possible relocation. Basically it is still a mystery what happened to this great civilization, which left behind massive stone temples, calendars, and of course, pok-a-tok courts that one can visit today.

The Aztecs

The Aztecs had a meteoric (super fast) rise to domination, and a spectacular fall at the hands of the Spaniards. Like the Maya, they were thought to be descendants of Asians who first migrated to and then settled in North America.

First off, the **Aztecs** never called themselves the Aztecs. They called themselves the Mexica, which is where Mexico gets its name from today (you will see that modern-day Mexico adopted a lot from this ancient civilization). They came from the land of Aztlan, the Place of White Heron, which is where the name Aztecs derived from.

This frieze that appears in the rotunda of the US Capitol building depicts Cortes and Moctezuma at the Aztec Temple in 1519. Architect of the Capitol, photo taken in 2011.

The Aztecs were polytheistic (believed in many gods) and part of their rise came from a belief that their god of war, Huitzilopochtli (say that ten times fast) sent them on a 100 year journey to find an eagle perched on a cactus on an island in the middle of a lake--with a snake in its talons. Which you generally come across once every, oh,100 years.

During their wandering in the desert, they came under the rule of the king of Colhuacan. The Aztecs orchestrated a marriage between the daughter of one of the lords of Colhuacan and an Aztec leader. Not knowing what would befall her, the lord sent his daughter to participate in the marriage ceremony. When he arrived, however, the Aztecs had ritually sacrificed and then skinned her, and a priest was dancing in his daughter's skin! Enraged, the Colhuacan troops chased the Aztecs to a swampy island in the middle of Lake Tezcoco, where, LO AND BEHOLD, in the middle of the water, they found their long awaited symbol - an eagle perched on a cactus with a snake in its talons. This is also the symbol you'll find on Mexico's flag today.

The year was 1325 when the Aztecs settled this island and founded their great city of Tenochtitlan, which grew to be the most densely populated city in Mesoamerica, with 150,000 people at its height.[51]

You may be wondering how this marshy island contained (and fed) that many people. The Aztecs worked diligently to build causeways to connect their island to the mainland, created sophisticated walls to prevent flooding, and built floating islands on which they grew their crops, called **chinampas**. They also were the first of the ancient civilizations to educate girls, though sometimes those girls ended up the subject of human sacrifice, which the Aztec, like the Maya, practiced regularly. By the time **Moctezuma** came to power in 1440, the Aztecs ruled between 5 and 6 million people, either by conquest or by taxing them heavily.

Life seemed to be going swimmingly for the Aztecs until 1519, when the Spanish conquistador (conqueror) **Hernan Cortes**, having heard rumors of this civilization from a previous explorer, arrived in Mexico. He had several advantages going for him. One was that the Aztecs had never seen horses before. The second was that an Aztec prophecy had predicted that the light-skinned god Quetzalcoatl would return at about that time. Third, the Spaniards brought with them guns and germs ~ two enemies that would mean the end of the Aztec civilization. Finally, the over 500 civilizations that had fallen under Aztec control were chafing at the harsh rule and ripe to be turned against them, an advantage that Hernan Cortes would successfully exploit.

At first Moctezuma greeted the visitors warmly. But Cortes was able to recruit a young woman from a neighboring tribe named **La Malinche**, who spoke both the Aztec language and Spanish and acted as his translator (and later wife). She was able to give Cortes valuable information about the plans and capabilities of the Aztecs.

Using his superior weapons, natives from rival tribes, and Moctezuma's mistaken belief that he was the returning god Quetzalcoatl, Cortes murdered thousands of nobles and took Moctezuma prisoner. He died in mysterious circumstances (some accounts say his own people stoned him to death after he tried to calm them on the orders of the Spaniards).

By 1521, 240,000 Aztecs were dead and the city of Tenochtitlan was under Spanish control. It would later become Mexico City, and the center of European domination in the New World.

The Inca

Though the Aztecs had the most populous empire, the title of the largest ancient Latin American civilization goes to the **Inca**. They were centered in Peru and Chile, in the Andes mountains. At their height, they were the largest single nation on earth!

If you have seen the Emperor's New Groove (and if you haven't, I recommend it!) you know that the center of the Incan empire was located in Cuzco. It expanded from Cuzco beginning in 1428 (so about the time that the Aztecs were exploding in Mexico).

Macchu Picchu, the most famous of all Pre-Columbian ruins, depicts the splendor of the Incan empire. Macchu Picchu remained undiscovered by Spanish conquistadors. Photo taken by Eduardo Zárate in 2008.

The three things that the Inca are most known for are: their 14,000 mile long road system that connected this huge empire, their worship of the Sun God, and their creation and dissemination (spreading) of a universal language, known as Quechua, that united their empire.

In the Incan society, work was a form of currency. There were no coins or dollar bills - subjects in the Incan empire paid "taxes" by laboring for the empire (often on their huge road system) and were paid in clothing or food. Silver and gold were abundant, but only used for decoration. Unfortunately, this abundance would be their downfall.

In 1532, the Incan empire had just recovered from a brutal civil war between **Atahualpa** and his brother, in which the former won by beheading the latter. This rift had weakened the empire significantly just as a new force was arriving on the scene.

Hearing of their riches, a Spanish conquistador named **Francisco Pizarro** arrived in Peru with a small army of a couple hundred men. Pizarro tricked Atahualpa into a "peaceful" meeting in which he ended up holding the king for a ransom. After giving up a room full of gold and other treasure to Pizarro, Atahualpa was strangled to death.[52] The Spaniards marched to Cuzco and conquered the rest of the civilization.

But this was a HUGE civilization, far more advanced than the Spaniards in their road system, irrigation, and tremendous wealth ~ how were they conquered by this small band of Pizarro's men?

The answer? DISEASE.

Diseases from Europe, from which there was no immunity in the New World, spread like wildfire. Smallpox in particular was devastating. The Incas, as a result, suffered terribly from the unfamiliar sicknesses brought by these strange men. Due in large part to disease, the native population of Latin America in the first 100 years after Columbus was reduced by 80-95 percent![53]

Most of the civilization was plundered by the Spaniards but one area, **Machu Picchu**, was left untouched due to its extreme elevation in the Andes ~ it wasn't "discovered" by Europeans until 1911. You have probably seen pictures of it before ~ many people travel to see the remnants of this highly advanced civilization that succumbed to the weapons and diseases brought by Pizarro and his men.

Section One Questions

1. Explain how humans first arrived in the Americas.

2. What is one significant attribute of each of the civilizations of the Maya, Aztec and Inca?

3. What advantages did the conquistadors have in fighting the natives? What advantages might the natives have had?

4. How did disease play a role in the history of Latin America's ancient civilizations?

4.2 The Era of Colonization

In Fourteen Hundred and Ninety Two, Columbus Sailed the Ocean Blue...and Discovered... millions of people living in North America and going about their business.

The first non-native people to find the so-called "New World" were likely the Vikings, who landed there in the 11th century. New evidence suggests that perhaps even the Chinese landed in the New World a few years before Columbus.[54] Instead,

what is important about this man is that he began a legacy of colonization and conquest of the New World by the Old, and an exchange of goods and ideas between them named the **Columbian Exchange** that would alter the course of history.

Columbus started life as **Cristoforo Columbo** - the Italian version of his name, as he was Italian-born. He was born in 1451, at the height of the "Age of Discovery" in which European powers were competing to "discover" new lands to profit from and colonize. The Portuguese were the first ones to start the trend, with the Spanish nipping at their heels.

Christopher Columbus. Sebastiano del Piombo, 1519.

The Spanish at the time were just finishing up a campaign called the "Reconquista" in which they were expelling all Jews and Muslims from the entire country. Once that task was complete, they turned their focus towards getting a hand in the riches of the Far East, particularly India. The trick was how to get there and back, fast.

Columbus was the son of a wool merchant, and began his career at sea in his teens. He survived the brutal takeover of one of his ships early on and floated on a piece of wood to Portugal, where he began in earnest his quest to become a ship captain, studying cartography (maps and map-making) and navigation. It was in Portugal that he got the idea that would alter the course of human history.

The big conundrum (problem) at the time in Europe was how to get to Asia quickly, where there were spices to be bought, riches to be discovered, and new foods to be brought back. A land route was long and dangerous. The Portuguese had figured out how to do this by circumnavigating (going around) the Cape of Good Hope in South Africa, and continuing on to Asia. Columbus argued there was a faster way ~ bypass the African continent altogether and go straight across the Atlantic!

Columbus's calculations, however, were a bit off. Oops. He believed the circumference of the earth was smaller than most other cartographers and scientists of the time believed - so he thought, ba-da-bing, bada-boom, sailing the Atlantic to Asia should be quick and easy. He presented this plan to the King of Portugal, but was rejected ~ instead, the Spanish court, under the rule of King Ferdinand and **Queen Isabella**, were intrigued - they wanted to find fame, fortune, and to export Catholicism to new lands - goals that lined up perfectly with that of Columbus. In exchange for 10 percent of the riches he found, Columbus set sail in August of 1492.

Three months later, Columbus believed he had hit Asia. Instead, he was in the Bahamas. He hopped around the Caribbean islands looking for the gold and riches he believed he would find, and when he came up empty-handed, he left a crew of 40 men behind in a trading fort in His-paniola (now called Haiti and the Dominican Re-public) and set sail back to Spain.

Queen Isabella II of Spain by Franz Xavier Winterhalter, 1852.

He made three more trips to the New World: still unsuccessful at finding riches, on his second trip he sent 500 slaves as a gift to Queen Isabella, who returned them, horrified.[55] On his third trip, the conditions at the fort in Hispaniola grew so bad there was a revolt, and Columbus was removed from the colony and thrown in jail back in Spain.

On his fourth and final trip he reached Panama, but came under attack from natives and lost two of his four ships. He returned to Spain mostly in disgrace.

The discoveries Columbus made eventually led to a rush of explorers heading to the New World. The exchange of fruits, vegetables, weapons, slaves, and diseases that began during Columbus's time is known as the Columbian Exchange, and resulted in a huge shift in the way Europe (and the New World) would cook, eat, live, and conduct war forever.

Treaty of Tordesillas

Two years after Columbus landed in the Bahamas, a treaty was signed between Spain and Portugal to prevent future conflict over the lands Columbus and other explorers had discovered and claimed for each throne. The treaty drew a line at approximately 50 degrees west ~ but the line was not always honored and was often extended. Essentially, Portugal gained control of Brazil, and Spain maintained a claim on the rest of Latin America ~ for a time.

Colonial Latin America: Who Rules?

Once these lands were claimed, there had to be some way to be sure each European country could maintain control over it. Each government set up systems to govern the people who came to the new lands seeking riches, as well as the people who were already there, bewildered by the imposition of these new folk.

Politically, the King and Queen were on top and maintained all of the power. But they were busy people. So they designated a **Council of Indies**, who also lived in the mother country (Spain or Portugal) and would make the major decisions regarding the governing of the colony.

Within the colony, a **viceroy** maintained control (he was the third rung of the political ladder). Beneath him was a **cabildo**, a local council that made laws that pertained to the local inhabitants in the colony.

Of course, all of these positions were held by whites who had immigrated from Europe. This created a social structure that was rigid and determined what job you could have, who you could marry, where you could live, etc. Whites who came over from Europe were called **peninsulares**. However, the children of peninsulares, born and raised in the colonies, had a lower social status - they were called **creoles** and often barred from those top political positions, like viceroy.

Below the creoles were the **mestizos** - people of mixed native and European blood. Many of the first immigrants to the new world were men ~ and many ended up with native wives or native mistresses, creating a whole new ethnic population.

Natives of course came next in the social hierarchy, followed by African slaves who had been brought over by Europeans to labor in the sugar cane fields and do other jobs that had decimated the native population. This group had the fewest rights and opportunities of them all.

Economics: The Mercantilism System

So what was the big draw of the colonies? Money of course! There was LOTS of money to be made over these formerly "unexplored" areas, and the most significant way to do it at this time was through **mercantilism**.

When you think about mercantilism, think about the word inside it: merchant. A merchant is someone who goes to the market to sell his or her goods at a higher price than they bought them or produced them for, and make a profit.

In mercantilism, the mother country (Spain or Portugal, generally) sought to take raw goods from the colony, ship them to Europe, turn them into more expensive finished goods, and sell them back to the colony. And just to make sure there's no competition, the colonies aren't allowed to build their own factories.

The idea is that raw goods (trees, cotton, for example) are much cheaper than the finished goods that took time, labor, and machinery to transform (trees into furniture, cotton into clothes). Therefore, the mother country took the raw goods from the lands they had claimed, turned them into finished goods in European factories, and sold them back at a high price to people with no other competing options. Mercantilism is one of the main ways Europe profited from the colonies - by exporting far more than they imported, and thus creating a favorable balance of trade.

Another way they profited ~ and got Europeans to settle and hold the land for them ~ was through the **encomienda system**. In the encomienda system, the King or Queen grants a European a certain number of natives to work for him with the idea of controlling the population and land surrounding it. In exchange, the European must provide food, shelter, and Catholic teachings to the natives. Everyone wins, right?

Wrong. Most of the natives were enslaved, beaten, rarely fed or clothed and certainly not taught Catholic beliefs. So many died in this system that a priest named **Bartolomé de las Casas**, who was living in Hispaniola and witnessing the abuses, appealed to the crown to stop using the encomienda system altogether.

Knowing that SOMEONE had to keep doing all the work, de las Casas suggested that Africans should be imported to work the fields since they were "used to" the tropical conditions and back-breaking labor.

Millions of them died in the same way, often earlier than the natives. For those living in the colony and doing the work to keep Europe's economy going full speed ahead, the struggle was real.

Section Two Questions

1. Explain why there might be controversy over the celebration of Columbus Day.

2. In what ways is Mercantilism present in other parts of the world?

3. How did the Columbian Exchange change both the new and the old worlds?

4. Explain how the colonies were organized and ruled, and what factors were mot important in determing one's status in the colony.

5. How was the encomienda system in theory different from the encomienda system in practice?

4.3 The End of Colonial Rule

Let's start with an acronym. By the late 1700s, the colonies in the New World were ripe for revolution. The four reasons can be summed up this way ~ complaints by those in the colonies were falling on DEAF ears.

First, there was a sense of **Disempowerment** in the colonies - those living in the colonies felt they had no political or social power - especially those who were not peninsulares. Creoles looked the same as the peninsulares, the only difference being that they were born and raised in the New World - and they were sick of playing second fiddle to the peninsulares. Political decisions still came from across the ocean or miles away from a viceroy who had no idea what was going on locally.

Second, a powerful set of ideas were spreading through Europe at the time - it was called the **Enlightenment**. These ideas were all about the rights of the people to choose their leaders, and marked a dramatic shift from a time when the people believed their leaders were chosen by God to rule. Now, the people were beginning to believe that the monarchy had a contract with the people - as long as they took care of the people's basic needs and respected their rights, the people would continue to keep them as rulers ~ once the people's rights and needs were ignored, it was the right of the people to rebel. This idea spread to the New World, where creoles, mestizos, natives, and African slaves began to absorb the idea that their rulers did not have their best interests in mind - and that revolution was a possibility.

Latin American years of independence by country. Joker92, 2007.

Third, the **American Revolution** of 1776 was inspirational to many living under the rule of Spain and Portugal in the New World. The Americans, a smaller and more poorly equipped force, had successfully and unexpectedly thrown off the British, the world's largest naval force. If the Americans could do it, those in the colonies thought, so can we. Such trend setters, those Americans!

Finally, the **French Revolution** of 1789 had brought Napoleon Bonaparte to power. Napoleon began a series of wars, known as the **Napoleonic Wars**, that raged throughout Europe and ended up putting his friends and family on the thrones of Spain, Portugal, Brazil, and Italy, among others. With the original monarchs thrown out by Napoleon, leaders in the New World saw the weakness of the Spanish empire and took the opportunity to strike.

The First Domino to Fall: Haiti

The United States was the first country in the Americas to achieve independence. Haiti was the second, in 1804. The former French colony, known as Santo Domingo, was the most profitable colony in the Americas, raking in millions for France as a producer of sugar and coffee. The huge production of these crops, however, required massive numbers of African slaves. After the French Revolution split the island's white minority into two groups, those in support of the revolution and those in support of the monarchy, the African majority sensed their opportunity and rebelled, in 1791. The rebellion was led by **Touissant L'Ouverture**, a self-educated former slave. This revolt would begin a war that would last 13 years, and would result in a messy series of conflicts between whites, slaves, free people of color, France, Spain, and Britain.

After France abolished slavery in 1794, Touissant turned against the Spanish allies he'd created on the other side of the island and fought to capture the neighboring colony (now the Dominican Republic). However, when Napoleon took control of France in 1799, he reinstated slavery in the colonies, captured L'Ouverture, and exiled him to an icy French prison, where he died. Haiti was finally liberated from French control in 1804, becoming the scene of the most successful slave revolt in world history and the first independent black nation in the Western world.

Miguel Hidalgo and the Cry of Dolores

"My children... Will you free yourselves? Will you recover the lands stolen three hundred years ago from your forefathers by the hated Spaniards? We must act at once... Will you defend your religion and your rights as true patriots?"

Miguel Hidalgo, painted by Antonio Fabres, 1992.

So began the famous Cry of Dolores, uttered by a creole priest, **Miguel Hidalgo**. This call to action began the Mexican War of Independence on September 16, 1810. Hidalgo united mestizos and creoles in a bloody war against the peninsulares who controlled the Spanish colonial government in Mexico. Like Haiti, it was a long and hard-fought battle that ended after Hidalgo's death, in 1821.

Following the Cry of Dolores, Hidalgo led a series of battles and amassed an army of 100,000 (though they were poorly armed, some with rocks and sticks).[56] The rebel army marched towards the capital in Mexico City, killing peninsulares as they went. Upon reaching Mexico City, Hidalgo had a great advantage in numbers, but for reasons historians are not sure of, he retreated. It gave time for the Spanish forces to refocus and eventually capture Hidalgo, sentence him to death, and execute him, with his head eventually hung in the city as a warning for those considering revolution.[57]

But the revolution would not die, and continued under the leadership of Jose Morelos (also captured and executed, in 1815). Finally, under the command of Agustín de Iturbide, Mexico gained independence, in 1821.

Simon Bolivar, the George Washington of South America

Meanwhile, in South America, a creole planter named **Simon Bolivar** was planning his own revolution. He would go on to liberate Venezuela, Colombia, Peru, and Ecuador from Spanish control. His intent was to create a **Gran Colombia** from Venezuela, Colombia and Peru, which he envisioned as a United States of Latin America. He was a huge fan of George Washington, and George Washington felt the same about him. The biggest difference was that Bolivar did not think they could achieve independence and maintain slavery, as the United States had.

Every time Bolivar liberated a country from Spanish rule, those he left in charge tried to consolidate their power in their own area, rather than adhering to his dream of Latin American unity. Unfortunately, fighting between representatives of each area prevented the formation of a unified government - and the dream of Gran Colombia failed as the countries separated once again.

The Rest of the Dominoes Fall

Jose de San Martin, a contemporary of Bolivar, liberated Argentina and Chile, and together with Bolivar liberated Peru. Instead of seeing a vision of a unified, democratic

Latin America, de San Martin looked towards old models of rule, such as dictatorship and monarchy. This rift would lead Bolivar to declare, with great sadness, "America is ungovernable for us. He who serves a revolution plows the sea."[58]

By 1825, most of Latin America was under the control of Latin Americans ~ mostly creole leaders of revolution. Cuba was the only major colony still under European control - and would stay that way until the Spanish-American War of 1898.

Section Three Questions

1. Compare and contrast the causes of the Latin American Revolutions (remember the acronym DEAF) with the causes of the Arab Spring and/or the Russian Revolution. Find three ways in which the Latin American revolutions were similar to either or both, and how they were different.

2. What were the causes of the revolt in Haiti? What role did the French Revolution have in creating opposing sides on the island of Haiti?

3. Why did Simon Bolivar's dream of Gran Colombia fail to succeed?

4.4 The First Tests of Independence

As Spain and Portugal lost influence in Latin America, two new powers were emerging to take their place ~ Britain and the United States. Seeing their opportunity, in 1823 the United States passed the **Monroe Doctrine,** saying "the American continents... are henceforth not to be considered as subjects for colonization by any European powers." With this document, the United States would introduce themselves as a dominant power in the region.

The U.S. learned from the Europeans and saw there was much money to be made in Latin America. It was still a young country, but had the backing of Britain, which also had an interest in keeping Spain and Portugal out of Latin America for good. The cycle of dependence on raw goods led to the continued growth of cash crops in Latin America, a lack of modernization and a dearth (lack) of factories. Latin Americans continued to rely on foreigners - now the United States and Britain instead of Spain and Portugal - for all their finished goods. This would continue the pattern of economic dependence Latin America had on Europe and the United States.

The Mexican-American War

In 1846, Mexico and the United States would begin a conflict that would last a mere two years, but would make 55% of Mexico into US territory, and change the fate of the two countries forever.

Texas is at the root of the conflict. It was a Mexican territory that was inhabited by Native Americans, and the government in Mexico City was concerned that it was losing its control over the territory to the natives without a proper Mexican presence. In a surprising move, they invited Americans to settle the land and "hold down the fort" for Mexico.

But soon, these Americans felt no allegiance to Mexico - or America. They felt allegiance to Texas, and wanted it to be its own republic, declaring its independence in 1836 (hence the nickname of Texas, the Lone Star Republic). Texas was annexed by America in 1845, further angering the Mexicans. President James K. Polk tried to buy

The loss of Mexican territories following the Mexican-American War included Arizona, Utah, Nevada, California, and parts of New Mexico, Colorado and Wyoming. Created and uploaded by Kballen, 2008.

the territories of California, New Mexico and land on the southern border of Texas for $30 million dollars. Mexico refused to even discuss it.

Polk believed in **Manifest Destiny**, the idea that Americans were meant to inhabit all of North America. This belief fueled him into sending American troops to Texas, over the disputed border with Mexico. Mexican troops retaliated, and Polk used it as an excuse to go to war on May 11, 1846.

The most famous Civil War generals, Ulysses S. Grant and Robert E. Lee would get their start in the **Mexican-American War**. Grant later declared that the war was "one of the most unjust ever waged by a stronger against a weaker nation. It was an instance of a republic following the bad example of European monarchies, in not considering justice in their desire to acquire additional territory." Though American troops were mostly outnumbered by Mexican troops, they fought with a well-organized and well-directed military. The war ended when American troops took control of the capital, Mexico City.

The **Treaty of Guadalupe Hidalgo** formally ended the conflict: it granted the United States the modern-day states of Utah, California, Nevada, New Mexico, and parts of Colorado, Oklahoma, Arizona and Wyoming. They gave up all claims to Texas as well. In exchange, the United States paid Mexico $15 million dollars.

The Spanish-American War

If you've ever heard of **Guantanamo Bay**, wondered why Puerto Ricans are US citizens but cannot vote in presidential elections, or been curious about our frosty relationship with Cuba, you may be surprised to learn that it all connects to one conflict that broke out between Spanish-controlled Cuba and the United States in 1898.

By the late 1800s, Cuba was one of the last Spanish-controlled territories in Latin America. Cubans began fighting for independence during the 1890s and found an unexpected ally when the battleship **USS Maine** sailed into the Havana harbor in 1898.

You see, American sugar companies were making a lot of money off of plantations in Cuba, and had sent the USS Maine to observe the fight between Cuban patriots and the Spanish army and provide an escape for American planters should they need an exit. The U.S. had been supportive of previous attempts by Cuban rebels for independence, but their support intensified after the USS Maine exploded mysteriously while docked in the harbor on February 15, 1898, killing over 260 American sailors.[59]

To this day, the cause of the explosion is unknown. The Navy launched a four week inquiry and declared that it had been a mine placed under the ship that had detonated. Much later, a different theory was postulated that coal in the bottom of the ship had spontaneously combusted. Neither theory has been proven.

Despite the lack of evidence, the United States newspaper industry, knowing that war sells newspapers, began reporting on stories of "the Butcher", a Spanish General whose starvation policy led to the deaths of 100,000 Cubans.[60] Many of the stories were fabricated to try to sway the American public towards war, and were labeled "**Yellow Journalism**".

Theodore Roosevelt, then the Assistant Secretary of the Navy (and later our 26th President) was more excited about war than almost anyone. Roosevelt resigned his position and began recruiting college friends, hunters, and Native Americans for a group that became known as the "Rough Riders".

Roosevelt led his regiment to two very decisive victories at San Juan Hill and Kettle Hill. During one of his charges, he drew a gun recovered from the USS Maine and shot a Spaniard. Within 10 weeks, the war was over. Spain's empire was dismembered, the United States' influence was on the rise, and Roosevelt's heroism in what Secretary of State John Hay called "the splendid little war" helped propel him to the White House.

William Barritt's cartoon mocks the yellow journalism used to sell the Spanish-American War. First published in Vim, 1898. Via the Library of Congress.

In addition to securing Guam, Puerto Rico, and the Philippines, the **Spanish-American War** also led the United States to leasing a permanent military base on Cuba called Guantanamo Bay, where the most dangerous suspects of terrorist activities are held today. The U.S. also forced the Cuban revolutionaries to include in their constitution the **Platt Amendment**, which granted the US the right to interfere in Cuba's affairs for thirty years. It left a bitter taste in some Cuban's mouths, who felt they had traded Spanish rule for American rule. This resentment would lead to the rise of Fidel Castro, and culminate in the terrifying **Cuban Missile Crisis** of 1962.

Section Four Questions

1. What is the Monroe Doctrine and what is its significance?

2. Think about all the changes that occurred to land, population, and resources due to the Mexican-American War. What lasting conflicts did this War create for Americans? What lasting conflicts did it create for Mexicans? List and explain at least two effects of the War for each side.

3. What was the role of the media (newspapers) in creating the Spanish-American War?

4. How did the Spanish-American War affect the relationship between the the United States and Cuba?

4.5 This is Bananas

Teddy Roosevelt wasn't done with his activities in Latin America. In the late 1800s, the United States offered to buy the rights to build a canal through Panama, which was then part of Colombia. The French had previously tried and failed, due to rampant disease ~ to do the same thing years earlier. However, when President Roosevelt offered Colombia $10 million to complete the canal, Colombia refused.[61] Feeling rebuked but not dissuaded, Roosevelt supported a group of rebels from the area of Panama to rebel and form their own country. He gave them the full weight of the US Navy.

There was no real battle. At most, it raged for a few hours. Colombian soldiers were paid $50 to put down their weapons.[62] A massive US battleship waited menacingly off the coast, just daring the Colombians to test them. In 1903, Panama became an independent nation. Construction on the canal began almost immediately.

But America was not done in its quest to establish and maintain influence in the region. Conveniently, Panama's constitution was already written ~ by Americans. The first efforts to build the canal were a miserable failure of epic proportions. The first man responsible for building the canal had no plan and no sense of how big the job was.

Three quarters of the Americans who came to build the canal left while he was in charge. The cost so far: 128 million dollars.[63] But there was cause for hope! The former chief engineer,

A cartoon depicting Teddy Roosevelt's efforts to build the canal. December 1903, by W. A. Rogers of the New York Herald via The Granger Collection.

Wallace, was replaced by the rugged and ingenious John Stevens. Stevens had built the

Great Northern Railroad across the Pacific Northwest and his arrival marked a turn in fortunes for the beleaguered canal. In rough territory from Canada to Mexico, he had proven his tenacity. Stevens saw the destruction that had been wrought by disease, and got to work draining swamps, paving roads, and dumping pesticides throughout the area, all in an effort to eradicate malaria-carrying mosquitoes that had doomed the first attempts.

The canal officially opened in August of 1914, but the world's attention was focused on Europe, where World War I was just starting to break out.

Stevens also set up a massive infrastructure to house, feed, entertain, and keep healthy those who came to labor in the canal. Since the Pacific Ocean is lower than the Atlantic Ocean, the engineers used locks to get boats across the canal. As boats floated from one lock to another, the water level rose or fell to propel it through the passage.

Tensions built gradually between Panamanians who believed the Canal Zone belonged to them and Americans who occupied and ran the 10 mile zone as a US territory. After tensions exploded on Martyr's Day in 1964, resulting in the deaths of 20 Panamanian students and 4 US soldiers, talks began about handing over control to the Panamanian government. Though a treaty was approved in 1979, it was not until 1999 that Panama regained control of the entire zone.

Banana Republics

Many of the smaller countries in Central America struggled greatly to form democratic governments in the post-independence era. The problems were a result of large amounts of land belonging to the very few and a huge proportion of the people not having any land of their own. Remember that Latin America missed out on the industrial era (building their own factories and modernizing) because mercantilism led them to become dependent on foreign companies. This continued into the 1960s and 1970s, and led to a startling trend: banana republics.

If you've been to a mall lately, you may recognize this phrase. Go into a Banana Republic store, however, and you will likely not get a straight answer from an employee about the store's namesake. That is because the meaning of this term is pretty controversial.

Bananas are not native to Latin America. They come from Asia, but early explorers found that they grew well in the sunny climate of many Central American countries, and began to plant bananas there. Bananas became very popular, particularly in the United States ~ they shipped well and were adopted as a healthy part of a child's school lunch. But **banana republics** became a symbol for the strength of United States businesses in weak Latin American countries, and their tendency to control not just the industries, but also the governments of those countries. When groups within banana republics tried to revolt, the US government often used the Cold War as a reason for interfering and putting down the rebellion.

Chiquita was once known as the United Fruit Company. Photo by photographer UggBoy UggGirl, 2009.

The Cold War and Latin America

Hopefully when you read "Cold War" it rung a bell for you from our Russia unit, but let me refresh your memory briefly. In the post-World War II era, there were only two superpowers remaining - the United States and Russia (known as the USSR or Soviet Union at the time). From 1945-1991, these two powers competed for influence throughout the world, and tried to spread their economic and political philosophies through violence, coercion, bribery, and alliances. The United States pushed capitalism in the areas it sought influence ~ the Soviet Union pushed communism. Latin America was of particular importance to both, as it was the neighbor to the powerful United States and brought the Cold War to a much hotter level every time the Soviet Union gained a foothold there.

Cuba was the feistiest of Latin American battlegrounds. The United States had maintained a very friendly relationship with the dictator **Fulgencio Batista**, who made the capital of Havana into a playground for the rich and famous of America with casinos, bars, and all night dance clubs. Meanwhile, landless peasants toiled in the countryside, and dissidents (those who spoke out against him) were cruelly repressed.

One of the dissidents, **Fidel Castro**, a young law student, began building a movement in the 1950s to overthrow Batista. In 1953, he and his band of followers over-

took a military training base called the **Moncada Barracks**, killing several of Batista's soldiers. Many of Castro's fighters were rounded up and executed ~ he fled to the mountains until he got a guarantee that if he returned to face trial, he would not be tortured.

Batista agreed to this demand and Castro stood trial, acting in his own defense. He was charged with leading the revolution and sentenced to 15 years in prison. Cuba's population was glued to the tri-

Fidel Castro arriving in Washington 1959. Warren K. Leffler, Library of Congress .

107

al, and Castro became a household name. After his sentencing, he famously proclaimed: "You may condemn me. History will absolve me!"[64]

Two years later, trying to calm the masses, Batista let Castro go free. He went right back to building his revolution, and on New Year's Day, 1959, he took over the capital and forced Batista to flee. He set about turning Cuba into a socialist paradise, and was able to achieve land reform, free healthcare, free education, and free public transport. But it came at a cost. Dissidents were imprisoned or killed, there were no freedoms of speech or of the press, and Cuba remained economically depressed, especially after the Soviet Union fell in 1991. But before that happened, Castro would challenge its powerful neighbor to the North ~ and bring the world closer to nuclear war than it had been before or since.

In 1961, a newly elected and very young President John F. Kennedy saw Castro as a communist threat, a veritable floating military base for the Soviets to use. He wanted Castro out of power - and fast. The CIA secretly trained an army of 1,000 Cuban exiles in a mission to overtake the island - but there was a leak, and somehow the secret plot reached Castro. As the exiles arrived on the beach of the Bay of Pigs, Castro's forces were ready. The exiles were captured and held for $50 million in ransom ~ and the US, and its young president, were humiliated ~ but not done trying to take him out. In total, there were 638 recorded assassination plots against Fidel Castro while he was in power.[65]

In 1962, the Soviet Union sent over nuclear warheads in oil tankers to be delivered to constructed missile pads in Cuba. American U-2 spy planes had discovered these sites in October of 1962 and the race was on to see which side would blink first. Castro, with hatred for America's imperialist Platt Amendment and military base compounded by the previous year's attempt to assassinate him, was quite willing to have Cuba destroyed if it meant destroying the United States as well. Kennedy had many options - invade Cuba, bomb Cuba, bomb the Soviet Union - but as you'll remember from earlier in our studies, he decided to set up a naval blockade to prevent the "oil tanker" from delivering its cargo. Eventually, in a trade that did not become public for years afterwards, Kennedy agreed to withdraw missiles in Turkey he had pointing at the Soviet Union if the USSR withdrew its missiles from Cuba. Kennedy also had to promise never to attack Cuba again. The world gave a collective sigh of relief as the Cuban Missile Crisis came to a close.

The year 2015 brought the most significant change in US-Cuba relations since the embargo (ban on trade) against Cuba began in 1960. President Obama announced in January that, effective immediately, trade and travel restrictions would be significantly loosened between the two countries. In April, Cuba was removed from the list of states that support terrorism. In August 2015, the two countries re-opened embassies in each other's countries. The US prison at Guantanamo Bay, America's continuing embargo and Cuba's record of human rights abuses continue to be areas of tension that may be harder to agree on than the newly legal (and very popular) imports of Cuban cigars to the United States and smartphones to Cuba. In 2016, Fidel Castro died of natural causes at age 90.

Some of the restrictions on US travel to Cuba and embargos on Cuban-military owned businesses were reimposed by President Trump, though as of the summer of 2020 the embassies remain open.

Section Five Response

1. It has become extremely expensive to ship goods through the Panama Canal in recent years. China has invested in building a wider, newer canal through Nicaragua, although there has been no progress on construction since the announcement was made in 2013. Looking at the history of the Panama Canal, what challenges can you predict in a Chinese-backed business building a canal through Nicaragua? Who will be the winners and losers of this new project?

2. The relationship between the US and Cuba is evolving quickly. Go to a trusted news source and report on what the most recent status is of the relationship between the two countries.

4.6 Latin America Today

Now that you have read about the crisis of democracy and the difficulties of creating a healthy economy, the challenges of international trade seen in the banana republics and the Panama Canal, and the delicate relationship between the US and Latin America, you may have some predictions of your own to make.

An American journalist, James Reston, once wrote, "Americans will do anything for Latin America except read about it." Well, at least you have now disputed that theory!- Congratulations. Below are ten observations about Latin America today.

1. Most of the governments of Latin America, with Cuba as an exception, are democratically elected in fairly free elections. That does not mean their governments do not act in a very authoritarian fashion.

2. Fidel Castro's death in 2016 raises new questions about Cuba's future, although his younger brother Raul retains power over the country. Although there have been positives about rule, such as free healthcare and education, many Cubans are excited about the coming changes now that the United States' decades-long embargo (ban on trade) with Cuba has ended.

3. Venezuela has been embroiled in crisis ever since the price of oil began to crash in late 2014. Irresponsible spending under the leadership of Hugo Chavez and his successor, Nicolas Maduro, has led to a deep economic crisis in Venezuela, with shortages of food, medicine, electricity and other basic necessities.

4. Brazil, as Latin America's largest country, has many indicators that it will be successful economically, but also many challenges, including high rates of crime, corruption and poor infrastructure, all of which became big topics of controversy during the 2014 World Cup and 2016 Rio Olympics, the first to be held in South America.

5. In 2014, Brazil, Chile, Costa Rica and Argentina had females as head of state.

6. Mexico continues to fight a bloody drug war, but much of the violence and instability has relocated to Honduras and Guatemala because of crackdowns. Much of the

immigration from Latin America has shifted from Mexico to Central America as a result of rising incomes and opportunities in Mexico, and declining quality of life in Honduras, Guatemala and Nicaragua.

The former President of Argentina, Cristina Kirchner, poses for a photo with the former President of Brazil, Dilma Roussef in 2012. Roberto Stuckert Filho, via PR.

7. Colombia, once thought of as the most dangerous country in the world because of its decades-long drug war, is slowly mending fences with its former drug cartels and rebels and is much safer, even attracting tourists to some of the regions formerly off-limits to foreigners.

8. Argentina is no longer plagued by massive inflation and deflation, but is not as economically strong as it could be due to a reliance on commodities, or raw goods.

9. Pope Francis of Argentina is the first pope from the region. Latin America, however, is slowly becoming less Catholic, although it is still the most Catholic region in the world.[66]

10. China is quickly replacing the United States as the major investor in new infrastructure projects in Latin America. This will change foreign relations, economics in the region, and culture.

Section Six Response

For homework, complete your list of "Top Ten Most Important Things" you learned about Latin America during this unit. Be sure to include the significance of the event/ person/place that you are listing. It will be fun for us to compare how we evaluated significance in this unit.

CHAPTER 5: CHINA

Hall of Supreme Harmony in the Forbidden City, built during the Ming Dynasty. This is where weddings took place for the Ming and Qing dynasties. Photo by See-Ming Lee, April 2014.

The world's most populous nation has had an uneasy relationship with the United States lately. But this civilization, which has the second largest economy in the world, dates back 5000 years. It is the birthplace of Confucianism, Taoism, paper, fireworks, ice cream, and perhaps the most influential of all inventions: gun powder. It is ruled by the largest communist party in the world, which describes its economy as "socialism with Chinese characteristics."[67]

5.1 The First Chinese Settlements

Archaeologists have uncovered evidence that Chinese civilizations were taking root 5,000 years ago. As you've seen from our previous studies, these ancient societies NEED water sources in order to settle down, grow crops to support a sedentary population, and then specialize into jobs. That's what happened with the Chinese in the Yellow River valley (also known as the Huang He).

The civilization that sprouted between 2500 BCE and 2000 BCE led to the world's most continuous culture, keeping records of their language, religion, politics, and myths that have maintained a consistency for a long, LONG time. As other civilizations came in contact with the Chinese, many of their traditions were adapted into Chinese culture, and the societies themselves often just became absorbed into Chinese culture, but the core of the Chinese traditions remained largely the same.

The written history of the Chinese begins at the **Shang** dynasty. A note about dynasties - they are ruled by a king (the Chinese called him an emperor) and last as long as there is a continuous ruling family in charge. Normally this meant as long as there were sons being produced (and an army of royal concubines generally insured this was the case) but there were a few female empresses during the time of the Chinese dynasties, and I'll be sure to mention them as we go on. The Shang are known for their creation of the writing system, which (though it has evolved and changed dramatically) still lasts to this day.

The **Zhou** dynasty is credited with developing the Mandate of Heaven~a brilliant idea that forced the Shang out of power and ushered in the reign of the Zhou family. Essentially, the **Mandate of Heaven** is a belief that Heaven decides what family is placed on the throne and can remove that ruling family through floods, famine, or war. The Zhou created this idea and explained that the Shang had inherited the Mandate of Heaven from the mythical Xia dynasty, which had lost it through corruption. The Zhou also explained that the Shang emperor was roasting and eating his opponents - and that Heaven (through floods, famine, and war) had decided it was time for a new ruling family ~ which is how the Zhou got to rule.

After the Zhou dynasty fell, China was plunged into 500 years of war between different states that claimed they had the Mandate of Heaven. They were only reunited by the fierce and brutal dynasty of the Qin, from which China gets its Western name.

Though the **Qin** dynasty only lasted 38 years, it was one of the most significant of all the Chinese dynasties because of what it was able to accomplish. During its reign, the emperor **Qin Shi Huangdi** (which means First Emperor), began the construction of the **Great Wall**, introduced **Legalism** (the idea that people only respond to rewards and punishments), burned Confucian texts, and tried to become immortal (live forever) by drinking lethal doses of mercury.[68] He also commissioned a massive tomb for himself (now a popular tourist site) complete with an estimated 8,000 life-sized Terra Cotta soldiers, all individualized with different faces, hair, and armor.[69] He believed this tomb would protect him in the afterlife ~ he probably wasn't expecting that it would land on the itinerary of thousands of foreign tourists.

The largest room of terra cotta soldiers in Qin Shi Huangdi's tomb. Dennis Jarvis, 2006. Shaanxi, China.

The **Han** dynasty set the pattern for most of China's history, reinstating Confucian ideals, and creating a system of governance based on meritocracy (how smart and hard-working you were, rather than who your parents were, etc.) During the Han dynasty, the highest honor was being employed by the government, and men would try their entire lives to pass a grueling, multi-day civil service exam to enter into the profession. The overwhelming majority of Chinese people identify as belonging to the Han ethnicity, which has its roots in this dynasty.

The **Sui** dynasty was short-lived, with only two emperors, but was responsible for re-uniting China after another long period of war using brutal Legalist tactics to control the population.

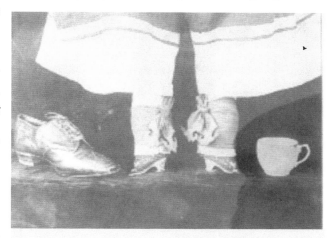

This photo shows the practice of foot-binding that became popular during the Song dynasty. To the left is an American woman's shoe, in the center the traditional lotus shoe, and a tea cup is shown for comparison. Otis Historical Archives National Museum of Health and Medicine, World War I era.

The **Tang** dynasty began the Golden Age in China - a time where math, science, and art saw major achievements, except under the harsh Empress Wu (of the Wu Tang clan!)

During the **Song** dynasty, the Golden Age was continued - many of the typically thought of attributes of Chinese culture emerged during this time. The Chinese began drinking tea instead of wine, replaced wheat with rice, developed the upturned roof as a style of architecture, and began the now frowned-upon practice of foot-binding, in which well-to-do women had their feet broken and bound from a young age to keep them impossibly small.

The **Yuan** dynasty was one of two not ruled by ethnic Chinese emperors - during this time, Genghis Khan's grandson **Khublai Khan** took over China and established the rule of the Mongols. Eventually, the Mongols adopted many of the Chinese customs and assimilated greatly into their culture.

The **Ming** dynasty marked a return to ethnic Chinese rule. They constructed the world's largest imperial palace, called the **Forbidden City**, and also finished the construction of the Great Wall that had begun under the Qin dynasty.

The final dynasty marked a return to foreign rule. The Manchus, from up north, established the final dynasty, the **Qing**, taking control from the Chinese. They began a descent into foreign domination when the British arrived in the 1600s. We'll cover that after we look at some of the fundamental teachings that have influenced Chinese history.

Section One Activity

1. Create a chart that lists all of the dynasties and what they are known for.

2. Note three similarities you can find between ancient Chinese civilizations and dynasties and the previous units on Africa, Russia, Latin America, and the Middle East.

3. Choose one of the dynasties that you believe was the most influential on China AND the rest of the world today. Explain three reasons WHY this is the most influential dynasty in your opinion.

5.2 The Fall of the Qing

There were many factors in the fall of the Qing - at least seven major events or people that led to the end of a 2,000 year long dynastic cycle and the beginning of a Republic. You can remember how the Qing fell by remembering this acronym: BOOSTER.

The Opium War & Treaty of Nanjing

By the early 19th century, cotton and opium from India had become the staple British imports into China, in spite of the fact that opium was prohibited in the country by imperial decree. In 1839 the Qing government, after a decade of unsuccessful anti-opium campaigns, adopted drastic laws against the opium trade. The emperor dispatched a commissioner to destroy 20,000 chests of illegal British opium.[70] The British retaliated, starting the first Anglo (British)-Chinese war, better known as the **Opium War** (1839-42). Unprepared and underestimating Britain's war capabilities, the Chinese were disastrously defeated.

The **Treaty of Nanjing** that following was called the "humiliating treaty": it gave British citizens extraterritoriality, or exemption from Chinese laws, five trading ports, ownership of the island of Hong Kong for 100 years, and payment for the destroyed

The signing of the Treaty of Nanking, by John Platt (painter), John Burnet (engraver), 1846.

opium. This treaty set into motion a series of events in which foreign powers gobbled up more and more of China's fragile sovereignty and trading supremacy.

The Taiping Rebellion: 1850-1864

A series of uprisings in the mid-1800's posed a serious threat to the survival of the Qing dynasty. The most important uprising was the **Taiping Rebellion**.

It lasted from 1850 to 1864 and cost millions of lives. The Taipings were a semi-religious group that combined Christian beliefs with ancient Chinese ideas for perfecting society. They challenged both the Qing dynasty and Confucianism with a program to divide the land equally among the people. During the rebellion, local Chinese officials organized new armies, which defeated the Taipings. The Qing received some military aid from the foreign nations that had signed the treaties. These nations wanted the dynasty to survive so the unequal terms of the treaties could remain in effect.

Empress Ci Xi

Empress Dowager **Ci Xi** (1835-1908) dominated the political life of China for nearly 50 years. She began as a concubine of the emperor, got promoted to wife for giving him a son, then ruled in place of her son when he was named emperor.

After her son's untimely death, she named (against the rules) her 3 year old nephew to the throne so she could continue ruling. As a ruler acting for child emperors, she and her cohorts brought a measure of stability to their nation. But, under her, the government was dishonest and did not make changes that were needed to benefit the people.

Empress Ci Xi (pronounced like SUH-SHI) refused to think about the necessary reforms suggested during the 100 days Reform. During the **Boxer Rebellion**, she claimed to support both

A photograph of Empress Dowager Cixi c. 1890 by Yu Xunling, then later colored in. The Empress is about 55 here.

118

the foreigners and the Boxers, and ultimately had to escape the Forbidden City dressed as a peasant woman to save her life. Her erratic rule eventually led to the end of the Qing Dynasty, which ruled from 1644 to 1911.

Spheres of Influence/Imperialism

Austria, France, Germany, Great Britain, Italy, Japan, and Russia all claimed exclusive trading rights to certain parts of China. They were dividing China into **"spheres of influence."** Some even claimed to own the territory within their spheres. By acquiring the Philippines in the Spanish-American War of 1898, the United States became an Asian power too. Now, with a strong base of operations just 400 miles from China, American businesses hoped to take advantage of China's vast resources. The foreign spheres of influence, however, threatened their ambitions.

The Failure of the Hundred Days' Reform

In the 103 days from June 11 to September 21, 1898, the Qing emperor, Guangxu (1875-1908), ordered a series of reforms aimed at making sweeping social and institutional changes. Influenced by the Japanese success with modernization, the reformers declared that China needed innovation, and institutional and ideological change. Opposition to the reform was intense among the conservative ruling elite, especially the Manchus, who bashed the announced reform as too radical, and proposed instead a more moderate and gradual course of change. Empress Ci Xi then carried out a coup d'etat and forced Guangxu into seclusion.

A cartoon from the French magazine Le Petit Journal in 1898 depicting the West's imperialist intentions towards China. Cartoon by Henri Meyer.

The Open-Door Policy

A disastrous war with Japan in 1894 and 1895 forced China to give up its claim on Korea.

China also had to give the Japanese the island of Taiwan, which the Qing had controlled since 1683. France, Germany, Italy, Japan, Russia, and the United Kingdom then forced the crumbling Qing empire to grant them more trading rights and territory. The division of China into a number of European colonies appeared likely. But the Chinese people had begun to develop strong feelings of national unity. This growth of nationalism helped prevent the division of the country, as did rivalry among the foreign powers. None of the foreign powers would allow any of the others to become dominant in China. Beginning in 1899, the United States gradually persuaded the other Western powers and Japan to accept the **Open-Door Policy**, which guaranteed the rights of all nations to trade with China on an equal basis.

Boxer Rebellion

In the summer of 1900 members of a secret society roamed northeastern China in large groups, killing Europeans and Americans and destroying buildings owned by foreigners. They called themselves the "Righteous and Harmonious Fists." They practiced boxing skills that they believed made them immune to bullets. To Westerners they became known as the Boxers, and their uprising was called the Boxer Rebellion.

Most Boxers were peasants or bandits from northern China who resented the growing influence of Westerners in their land. They organized themselves in 1898, and in the same year the Chinese government~then ruled by the Qing Dynasty~secretly allied with the Boxers to oppose such outsiders as Christian missionaries and European businessmen. The Boxers failed to drive foreigners out of China, but they set the stage for the successful Chinese revolutionary movement of the early 20th century. So remember the Booster shot that ended dynastic rule: Boxer Rebellion, Opium War, Open Door Policy, Spheres of influence, Taiping Rebellion, Empress Ci Xi, and the Reform failure.

The Republic of China

With the Qing gone, who would rule? There were two choices in 1911 that emerged to take power: the **Nationalists**, called the Guomindang or GMD, and the **Communists**, called the Chinese Communist Party (CCP).

At first, both parties tried to work together to get the other party to join them. For a while, between 1928-1949, **Chiang Kai-Shek**, leader of the Nationalists/Guomindang, ruled the country.

After failing to woo the communists, he chased them out of his government, then across the country, in what was called the **Long March from 1934-1935**. Kai-Shek's goal was to get rid of all of the communists. So, led by a new leader named **Mao Zedong**, the Communists began a 6,000 mile journey from Southeast to Northwest China.

The chase lasted over a year. Of the 86,000 communists who joined the march, only 8,000 survived to the end.[71]

The communists remained in Northwest China, trying to regain strength. But an outside power would soon push the two opposing sides together.

In 1931, Japan (the aforementioned outside power) seized Manchuria, the northern-most part of today's China. In 1937, Japan, struggling to pay off its debts from the Great Depression by expanding its territory, launched an all-out war on China. When World War II arrived, the Nationalists and the Communists joined together briefly to battle their common enemy: Japan.

In 1945, Japan was defeated when the US dropped two atomic bombs on the mainland cities of Hiroshima and Nagasaki. At the end of the massive conflict, Mao and the CCP controlled the North, while the Guomindang held the South. Although the conflict had briefly united the two warring factions, the end of the war brought the two parties back into conflict. The Guomindang was backed by the US, while the communist Soviet Union backed the CCP. The Guomindang's army suffered from poor morale, low rations, and poor pay, while the communists were disciplined, paid well, and attracted the attention of the peasants, for whom their message of land reform and free education rang very true.

In 1949, the Communists swept into Beijing. The Guomindang's leadership, including Chiang Kai-Shek, fled to Taiwan, declaring itself to be the legitimate voice of the Chinese people. Meanwhile, Mao announced the birth of the **People's Republic of China**, beginning the Communist era.

Section Two Activity

1. Draw a diagram or write two paragraphs explaining how the Qing dynasty fell. There are at least seven factors at play here - be sure to include them all and describe how they may have contributed to the fall of the final dynasty.

2. Compare and contrast the Communists and Nationalists in China, and reference an example of a similar political or religious conflict that split a country into two from one of our earlier units.

5.3 Mao in Charge

Mao Zedong's official portrait by Zhang Zhenshi.

The Communists seized power over China on October 1, 1949. Immediately, Mao tackled two problems that had beleaguered China under Chiang Kai-Shek: hyperinflation and land reform. In China, like in Latin America, very few people, called landlords, owned most of the land, and the peasants worked the land with little to no hope of economic mobility. Their slogan, echoing that of the Soviet Union's decades earlier, was "Land to the Tiller!"

The policy of **land reform** was pretty brilliant because 80% of the country was made up of landless peasants, who obviously supported this reform.[72] Some peasants sought revenge on the landlords and over one million people died in the transition. Those who were suspected to have been too eager to seek revenge were removed from the Chinese Communist Party (CCP).

In addition, Mao appealed to half of the population by passing the **Marriage Law**, allowing women to divorce their husbands for the first time. This led many women to escape oppressive and abusive relationships ~ and turn their gratitude towards Mao.

China was still largely agrarian ~ the Industrial Revolution had not quite hit them yet. The CCP saw the countryside as a way to advance and in fact, industrialize the economy. China's economy had been wrecked by years of civil war and war with the Japanese, as well as participation in the Korean War from 1950-1953.

With this in mind, the CCP began the first in a series of grand industrialization plans. This part should sound a bit familiar. In 1953, the first major economic plan was announced - a massive industrialization plan that would transform China into an industrial powerhouse in ~ you guessed it ~ five years.

However, poor weather led to bad harvests in the first few years of the new plan. A new plan was proposed, which should sound familiar: **collectivization**.

123

There was less resistance in China to collectivization than there had been in the Soviet Union. Collectives in China had about 170 families in them, and there was still some individuality allowed in terms of growing one's own food on private plots and living in separate houses. Progress was not moving fast enough, however. Mao felt more drastic measures would be needed.

Mao believed in the power of the masses ~ especially the masses in the countryside. So to empower the peasants, his traditional base, and to jump start economic growth, he introduced his most ambitious industrial program yet, in 1958: **The Great Leap Forward**.

The plan began by replacing collective farms with **communes** ~ a more extreme and Marxist vision of farming. Rather than 170 people living on a collective, an average of 5,000 people ate, lived, and worked all together.[73] Tools, animals, even personal property became the property of all in the commune. All across China, new infrastructure was built~mostly by hand. Roads, bridges, and dams sprung up all over the country. In addition, Mao announced a "battle for steel" in which regular peasants built furnaces to produce steel in their own backyards.

There was one problem: while all of this (low-quality, mostly unusable) steel was being produced, the seeds were not being sowed, and harvests were going uncollected. In addition, Mao put his two cents in to how the country's farmers should be doing their job. However, Mao himself had never run a farm. He had no idea what he was doing.

One of his disastrous suggestions was to kill all the sparrows, which Mao believed were eating the crops. In reality, the sparrows were eating the bugs that were eating the crops. So schoolchildren, armed with slingshots, took to the fields to destroy the sparrows. In doing so, it unleashed an infestation of crop-destroying bugs on China's fields.

Good weather helped keep the disaster at bay in 1958, but bad conditions led to a poor harvest in 1959, and typhoons in the south coupled with dry conditions in the north led to massive starvation in 1960. Commune leaders inflated the amount of food being produced, and distributed food to their families and friends, while others starved. With each year that passed, agricultural production plunged, and starvation, particularly in the countryside, worsened. Fertility rates plunged.

The Communist party blamed two foes for the famine that resulted: the weather and the

Soviet Union. The Soviets had withdrawn their advisors and equipment with the failure of the plan, and made an excellent scapegoat. By the end of 1960, it is estimated that between 15 and 30 million people had died from the catastrophic Great Leap Forward.[74]

The Great Proletarian Cultural Revolution

Following the disastrous Great Leap Forward, Mao took a back seat to ruling China. More freedom was given back to skilled managers and local communes. Some land even went back to private ownership, where it could be more effectively managed.

With the help of good weather in 1962 and the more pragmatic leadership of Mao's second-in-command, Zhou Enlai, China's economy recovered somewhat. Over the next four years, China gradually moved away from the brink of economic disaster.

This is the moment when Mao decided to begin plotting his return to power.

At 72 years old, Mao was no spring chicken. He complained bitterly about the bureaucrats that had taken control of China, and suspected that members of his own party were being influenced by counterrevolutionaries, bourgeoisie, rightists, and "capitalist roaders".

Mao sought to reestablish himself as the leader of the country through what is now known as the **Great Proletarian Cultural Revolution**.

The cover of non-copyright elementary school textbook from Guangxi in 1971, depicting three of Mao's Red Guards. Uploaded by Villa Giulia.

Beginning in 1966, Mao singled out elements of Chinese society as "Four Olds", meaning old ideas, customs, habits, and culture that needed to be eliminated. These were dangerous parts of society that lingered from the past, getting in the way of the progress of a socialist society. The chaos that unfolded would target landlords, rich peasants, teachers, skilled and educated workers, xenophiles, and anyone suspected of having an anti-Communist influence.

The schools were ground zero for the social and political revolution Mao intended to enact. Textbooks were thrown out and replaced with one **"Little Red Book"**, a small volume of Chairman Mao's quotes that children were expected to have with them at all times. Teachers were forced to radically overhaul and limit what they taught their students.

Students were encouraged to join the **Red Successors, Red Guard,** and later, the **Red Army** to show their devotion to Mao and cement their status as loyal communists.

The two years following the announcement of the Cultural Revolution were the most chaotic: some schools had to close because students were out participating in the revolutionary activities that they were encouraged to prioritize over their studies. The revolution did not officially come to an end until 1976, but by then a generation of schoolchildren had missed out on their most formative education years, jobs had been lost, lives had been ruined, and Mao was back on top~until he died later that year from his third heart attack, at age 82.

China and the Rest of the World

Since 1911, China has undergone two major revolutions. The first overthrew 2,000 years of dynastic rule. The second established communism in the world's most populous country.

Since then, the People's Republic has undergone several shifts in foreign policy.

At first, China's natural ties with the Soviet Union worried the United States deeply. America wanted to continue believing that the real Chinese government was just taking a leave of absence in Taiwan. Fortunately, the American government was able to see the reality of the situation, and in 1971, President **Richard Nixon** made a calculated move. While China and the Soviet Union were experiencing a massive rift, Nixon took the opportunity to approve a trip by the US ping-pong team to China. The following year, he expressed a desire to visit the People's Republic himself. Mao replied that he should come on over, and in 1972, Nixon and his wife caught a plane to Beijing.

Mao meets Nixon, 1972, from the U.S. National Archives and Records Administration.

When Mao met Nixon, the language barrier was amplified by the fact that Mao's translators were very nervous about misinterpreting anything the great leader said. So although not many words were exchanged, "Nixon Goes to China", as the visit became known, helped to thaw the Cold War-induced tension between the two countries quite a bit.

China's relations with the West took a dramatic turn in 1989, when calls for greater freedoms began in **Tiananmen Square**, in Beijing, after the funeral of a popular liberal reformist leader.

University students made up the bulk of the protesters, asking Chinese leader **Deng Xiaoping** to allow for greater freedom of speech and press and an end to rampant corruption in the government. At the height of the protests, nearly a million students filled the square.

Rather than acquiescing to these demands, tanks from the People's Liberation Army rolled into Tiananmen Square and cleared out the protesters by force on June 4th, 1989. Early estimates from the Chinese Red Cross, which were later retracted, put the death toll at 2,600, but no formal reports were ever released by the Chinese government. A declassified cable from the British Ambassador to China, revealed in 2017, put the estimate much higher, at over 10,000 dead. [75]

A North Korean celebration of their strong relationship with China in 2010. Taken by Roman Harak via Flickr Creative Commons.

Trade between China and the West soared in the 1990s and continues to play a major role in relations today, which is part of the reason the United States tiptoes around the delicate issues of minority rights in the far-west provinces of Tibet and Xinjiang, access to information on the internet, and human rights. However, in 2018, President Trump announced a slate of tarriffs (taxes on imports) to be imposed on Chinese goods. The Chinese government responded with their own set of tarriffs. It is still too soon to tell what the impact may be on either country's economy.

China's role as a mediator between the United States and North Korea has taken on greater importance in recent years. China supports the communist state of North Korea, which has made threats against the South as well as the United States, and has some nuclear capabilities.

Will the economic growth that has created a healthy middle class in China lead to political changes in the "Central Kingdom"? The current General Secretary of the Chinese Communist Party and President of the People's Republic of China, Xi Jinping, has not made any moves that would suggest that further political liberties are coming any time soon. In February 2018 he announced he was changing the constitution that would have limited him to two terms. Does this sound similar to any other leaders we studied this year?

Finally, in late 2019, in the Chinese province of Wuhan, an outbreak of the novel coronavirus which leads to the disease called COVID-19 began. This virus has spread throughout the world, leading to a massive global death toll, historic economic damage, and increased tensions between many countries, including China and the United States. The true toll of this pandemic will not be known for some time.

Section Three Activity

1. Explain how Mao changed China economically, socially, and politically. Include the Great Leap Forward, Cultural Revolution and President Nixon in your response.

2. Compare and contrast the experience of the Soviet Union under Stalin and the People's Republic of China under Mao Zedong.

3. Compare and contrast China under Mao Zedong and China under Deng Xiaoping. Which leader do you think has had a more significant impact on China?

CHAPTER 6: INDIA

A family visits the majestic Taj Mahal, the world's most beautiful tomb. Taken by Panoramas in 2009. *India was the first place humans are believed to have settled after Africa. As the birthplace of Buddhism, Hinduism, Jainism, and Sikhism, India is a vibrant nation with an incredibly diverse history. It is also a land of contrasts. Though it is the world's largest democracy, stories of political corruption dominate the news. Though many of the world's largest religions began here, conflicts between groups has ripped it into two countries (mostly-Muslim Pakistan was part of India until 1947). Named the "jewel" in the British crown as a colony due to its wealth of resources, desperate poverty afflicts millions of men, women, and children across the nation.*

129

6.1 Indus and India, Indeed

The story of India actually begins in its modern-day neighbor—Pakistan. The first Indian civilization began in the **Indus** River valley (from which India gets its English name). The first city, named **Harappa**, was built in this river valley in 2600 BCE. Harappa was an elaborate city, with a unified government that made sure that there was organization of construction down to the size of the bricks (all uniform, all the same). This civilization was emerging at around the same time the Egyptian, Chinese and Mesopotamian societies were forming, and many of their adaptations and developments are similar. Keep a close eye on the parallels between these civilizations.

The Indus civilization was thought to have fallen due to the arrival of the **Aryans** (meaning "the noble ones"), from Central Asia. These warriors introduced the caste system to India as well as some of the precursors (beginnings of) **Hinduism**. They wrote in the language of **Sanskrit** and recorded the **Vedas**, the most sacred of the Hindu holy books.

Hinduism is very different from the other religions we've studied this year. It is thought to be the world's oldest surviving religion, it has no one founder or place of worship, no one holy book, and no one god (it's polytheistic, meaning Hindus worship many gods). Even the word Hindu can be traced back to the Indus civilization, as Hindu is the Persian word for the Indus River.

All gods within Hinduism are today considered manifestations of Brahman, but there are three main deities: **Brahma**, the creator, **Vishnu**, the preserver, and **Shiva**, the destroyer.

Hinduism also lends a social structure to any society. Hindus believe you are born into your caste ~ your place in society. Strict adherence to this caste system means you can only do jobs assigned to your caste, only marry within your caste, and only associate with members of your caste. This is less true today than it has ever been, especially in cities and among young people ~ however, this is only a recent development. For thousands of years, the caste system has dictated life in India.

Doing your duty (**dharma**) well is extremely important ~ in fact, it is more important to do your duty poorly than to do someone else's duty well. **Karma** (you may have heard of this before) is how your actions in this life will affect you in the next life, and **Moksha** is breaking the cycle of reincarnation ~ a goal all Hindus aspire to, as the cycle can last a long, LONG time.

The Mauryans, Golden Guptas, and Delhi Sultanate

The Aryans were replaced by other foreign invaders, first the Persians from the West, and then the Macedonians, led by Alexander the Great. When Alexander the Great died, a power vacuum was left that was filled by a man named Chandragupta Maurya, who began the **Mauryan** dynasty. The first emperor of the Mauryans was Chandragupta Maurya, and during the Mauryans reign they ruled all of India except the southern tip. This dynasty ruled for 140 years, building a huge army, establishing a system of tax collection, and leaving a legacy with the reign of **Ashoka**, their most famous emperor.

Ashoka and the Buddha. AK Rockefeller, 2012.

Ashoka converted to Buddhism after the bloody **Battle of Kalinga**, and emphasized love and tolerance, even for those he conquered. He set up rest areas and paths to important Buddhist sites and encouraged conversion, but never forced it upon his subjects.

During the **Gupta** empire, which followed the Mauryan dynasty, India (like China's Tang and Song dynasties) experienced its Golden Age, in which trade with the outside world and scholarship grew enormously.

Muslim invaders overtook the Hindu dynasties in 1192 CE, founding a sultanate (kingdom) at **Delhi**: hence, the name of this dynasty is the Delhi sultanate. They destroyed Hindu temples as they invaded, but later they were more tolerant of different religions.

Most of the invasions occurred in the North (which makes sense geographically, since its borders are all northern). The South maintained small Hindi kingdoms at the same time.

The Mughals, aka the Mongols

In 1526, Mongols (the same ones who invaded China and maintained one of the largest contiguous empires in history) invaded from Northern India and founded the **Mughal** empire. Mughal is the Persian word for Mongol. Their rule spread over all of Northern India, Afghanistan, Pakistan and Bangladesh.

They had a passion for architecture, creating the enormous Red Fort at Delhi and the magnificent **Taj Mahal**, which draws millions of tourists to it each year.

Babur was the first emperor. Much of what we know about him comes from his autobiography, based on journals he began at age 10 and continued to write until his death. He was a successful military genius for sure, but also a poet and gardener. He was ruthless in battles, writing once: "Faced with our encircling attack, the Afghans could not fight...One to two hundred of them were captured to be slaughtered. Some were produced alive before us, but in most cases only their heads were brought to us. Those Afghans who had been brought to us as prisoners were ordered to be beheaded. Later a pillar of their heads was erected in our camp."[76]

His grandson, **Akbar**, who became the ruler of the massive empire at age 13, is considered by many historians to be the greatest of the Mughal emperors (hence his name, Akbar the GREAT). Though he was illiterate (could not read or write), Akbar made sure he was well-educated, bringing scholars in math, science, history, politics, and art to the palace to school him in all their subjects. He did not care if they were Hindus, Muslims, Sikhs, or atheists, he invited all into his court.

At a time when Muslims and Hindus had a rocky relationship, he married a Hindu princess and ended taxes on non-Muslims.[77] He realized there were too many Hindus to try to convert them to Islam, so instead, he made huge efforts to reconcile Hindus and Muslims. Akbar also gave land to the Sikhs (a relatively new religion that combined Hinduism and Islam) to build a Golden Temple in their holy city of Amritsar.[78] Akbar gained control through his acceptance of all religions, but was not afraid to use brutal means to crush any rebellion or refusal to submit to his rule. So, in the end, he was a very religiously tolerant guy~that is, as long as you're willing to live under his rule.

Shah Jahan, Akbar's grandson, famously built the Taj Mahal for his beloved wife, Mumtaz, after she died giving birth to her FOURTEENTH child. The Taj Mahal is her final resting place and took 22 years to complete. When Shah Jahan fell ill in 1658, it spawned a frenzy of activity among his sons, who began a series of wars to succeed him. His third son **Aurangzeb** defeated his brothers, declared his father incompetent to rule and imprisoned him in the Agra Fort. The Mughal empire ended in 1858 when the British officially took control, although it began crumbling in the 1600s as European weapons technology began to supersede that of the Indian military.

Section One Questions

1. How is the story of India's first civilizations similar to that of other regions we have studied this year? How is it different?

2. What different religions and origins did each dynasty contribute to modern India? What predictions might you make about modern India based on the early conflicts between groups?

6.2 The British Are Coming!

Starting in 1600 CE, the **British East India Company** (BEIC) started trading with India in goods such as spices, silk and tea.

By 1700 the BEIC had set-up three trading posts, in Bombay, Madras and Calcutta. The BEIC was like Walmart with an army. They were given a charter by the British crown to purchase territories, mint money, raise and command troops, form alliances, make war and peace, and be in charge of civil and criminal law in the acquired lands.

But the British were still competing with other European nations and trading companies for influence in India. After 1700 the East India Company faced many problems.

One was that British Christians were trying to change Indian customs, including **Sati**. Sati is a Hindu custom (rarely seen today) that is believed to have originated 700 years ago. After their husbands were beaten in battle, women would throw themselves onto a funeral pyre to avoid being taken as prisoners.

In later years the custom became seen as a symbol of devotion to one's husband - but sometimes she was tied up by her family and burnt against her will.

In 1829, following demands by Indian re-

Head of the BEIC Robert Clive and Mir Jafar after the Battle of Plassey, 1757 in which the BEIC expanded their influence in India. Painted by Francis Hayman, circa 1670.

formers, the British outlawed the practice. Many Indians were outraged by the cultural change the British were forcing upon them.

Though this practice still occurs, it is extremely infrequent (once every few years) and causes uproar in India and the rest of the world.

The British also rid the countryside of Thuggee (where the name "thug" comes from), roaming bands of thieves that made the countryside very dangerous for Indians traveling or living rurally.

Most importantly, however, was this idea that the British East India Company had an army ~ an army of Indian soldiers (called **sepoys**) - who were working for extremely low pay. Following cuts to their salary, the sepoys also were being forced to travel and fight abroad, which for Hindus meant losing their caste and starting over when they arrived back in India.

The last straw was a rumor that new bullet casings were being greased with pig and cow fat to make the bullets go into the barrel of the guns more smoothly.[79] Cows are sacred to Hindus, and pigs are considered unclean for Muslims ~ therefore, this rumor was egregiously offensive to both religions.

In 1857, the sepoys had had enough. Near Delhi, a group of sepoys murdered their British officers and a revolt started against the British that spread across India. The most brutal revolt occurred in the city of Cawnpore, where hundreds of British men, women and children were killed, some very brutally. The British would ensure they got their revenge.

After putting down the revolt, British soldiers made any sepoy suspected of being a rebel lick the ground where the British casualties had occurred at Cawnpore. Then, some rebels were tied to the mouths of cannons (see picture) and blown to pieces when the cannons were set off. [80]

Thousands died on both sides, and the relationship between the British and the Indians was forever altered.

The British government was horrified by the **Sepoy Rebellion**. They revoked the East India Company's charter and took control of the country. From 1858 on, the British government would rule India. This period became known as the British Raj (raj meaning rule in the Hindi language).

So why, in a country where Indians far outnumbered the British, did the Sepoy Rebellion fail and what were the outcomes? First, weak leadership of the rebellion and splits between Hindus and Muslims caused it to ultimately fail. The rebellion increased distrust between the British and the Indians, and led to the transfer of power from company rule (BEIC) to the British Raj. Finally, it officially marked the end of the Mughal Empire, which was on its last legs anyway, but which had suffered from indecision in who to support in the rebellion. You can remember the effects of the Sepoy Rebellion using the acronym FITE (Failure of the Rebellion, Increased distrust, Transfer of power from BEIC to the Raj, and the End of the Mughals).

This is a black-and-white reproduction of *Blowing from Guns in British India*, a painting created by Vasili Vereshchagin in the 1880s. Sepoys accused of participating in the rebellion were sometimes punished by being strapped to live cannons and shot from them. The Sepoy Rebellion signalled the end of the reign of the British East India Company and the Mughal dynasty.

Life Under the Raj - 1858 to 1947

The thing about educating people is that they often times learn "stuff" you aren't sure you want them to know. This was true of British rule over India. Elite Indians who formed the middle classes spent time studying in European schools abroad, and as a result, some became nationalists, people with intense pride in their country and a love of nation above all other ties. These new nationalists were proud of their Hindu heritage, wrote in English and their native languages, and emphasized Indian traditions over Western ones. In 1885, a group of nationalists formed the **Indian National Congress**, which would nurture and produce India's most famous national heroes.

However, they also overlooked potential Muslim leaders, which led to a split and the eventual formation of the **Muslim League**. Later on, the Muslim League would argue for their own country, and succeed in gaining one with the creation of Pakistan in 1947.

Mohandas Gandhi (1869 - 1948)

"Known as '**Mahatma**' (great soul), Gandhi was the leader of the Indian nationalist movement that fought against British rule, and is widely considered the father of his country, which is why he is often referred to as "Bapu", meaning father. His doctrine of non-violent protest to achieve political and social progress has been hugely influential, not just in India, but in the United States and South Africa as well.

Mohandas Gandhi was born in 1869 into the **Vaisya** (merchants) class. After university, he went to London to train as a lawyer. Unable to find a job in India, he went to work at an Indian firm in South Africa. Gandhi had not expected that Indians would face such intense discrimination in South Africa, and began a movement to protest Pass Laws that required every Indian to carry an identification card with him at all times.

His movement became quite popular and was successful at getting the white-minority government to drop many of the restrictive laws against Indians. He developed the idea of **satyagraha**, or devotion to truth, over his 20 years there, combining Hindu, Jain, and Christian beliefs in a prescription for addressing the wrongs of society in a nonviolent way.

When Gandhi returned to India in 1914, he was already gaining quite a reputation amongst Indians as well as amongst the British colonial authorities. He began to become involved in the Indian National Congress, an organization that had been the voice of India's elite since 1885.

Gandhi was not at first convinced that the British needed to leave India. It was not until after a violent reaction to a peaceful gathering of Sikhs in the city of Amritsar that Gandhi began to demand the British leave ASAP.

The **Amritsar Massacre** of 1919 began when Sikhs from all over India convened in their holiest city for a traditional fair, not knowing that the previous day the British had banned all gatherings. When the Sikhs gathered on the square, the British begun firing at them, killing 379 unarmed Indians. [81]

Gandhi as a young lawyer in South-Africa, 1906.
Photographer unknown.

By 1920, Gandhi was the most influential figure in Indian politics. He transformed the Indian National Congress into a voice for decolonization and his program of non-violent non-cooperation with the British included a campaign to make **homespun**, handwoven cloth that was traditional in India, rather than buying British goods.

In 1922, the British government decided that enough was enough and sentenced him to six years in prison. He was let out early but did not reenter the decolonization or **Home Rule** movement again until 1930, when he began an ambitious **Salt March** to protest the British tax on salt.

Gandhi led thousands of protesters on a 240 mile march to gather and make salt from the seawater.[82] British officials were incensed and again threatened to imprison the nonviolent resistance leader.

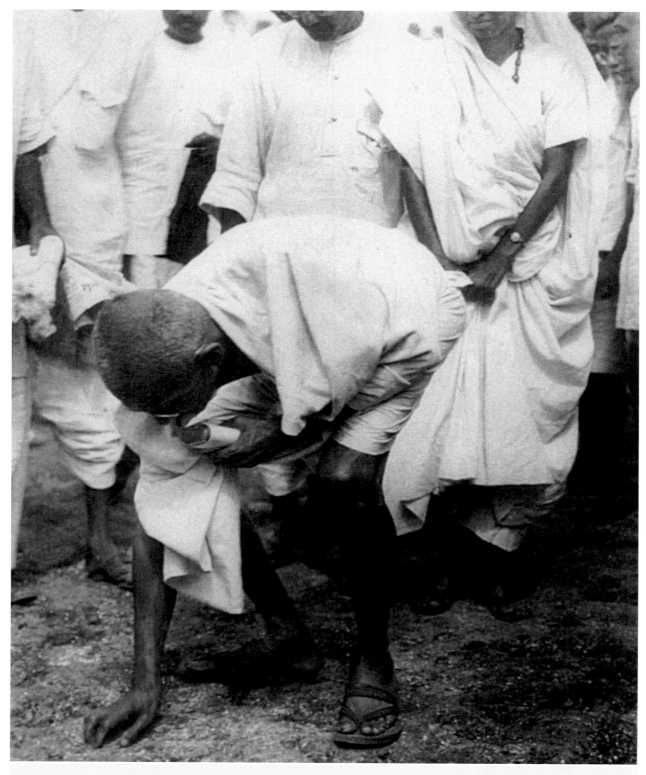

Gandhi at Dandi at the end of the Salt March. April 5, 1930, photographer unknown. His second son Manilal is standing behind him.

In 1931, Gandhi was invited to discuss India's independence at the **Round Table Conference** in London. Though Gandhi received a warm welcome from the British people, he left with no guarantee of independence for India.

As we saw in the case of many African countries, the final push for independence was helped along by outside factors, namely World War II. In 1945, the British government was recovering from the war's massive devastation that had sapped its finances and its military strength. The British government, Indian National Congress, and Muslim League all agreed on the **Mountbatten Plan** of June 1947, which created an independent India for Hindus and an independent Pakistan for Muslims. **Jawaharlal Nehru**, a prominent member of the Indian National Congress, became the first Prime Minister of India. **Muhammed Ali Jinnah**, the founder of the Muslim League, became the first Prime Minister of Pakistan.

This division became known simply as the Partition, and Gandhi hated it. Violence broke out all over the country as Muslims fled to Pakistan fearing violence if they remained in India and Hindus fled to India fearing the same. Gandhi began his longest fast in protest of the turmoil and attacks, which did succeed eventually in reducing the violence as Gandhi neared death from starvation.

Though he survived his final fast, on January 30, 1948, he was assassinated in Delhi by a Hindu fanatic who feared Gandhi was giving too much to Muslims in Pakistan. Unfortunately, this should sound a little bit like when Prime Minister Yitzhak Rabin was killed by a Jewish student who disliked Rabin's compromises with the Palestinians. Sometimes compromise and acceptance of difference is the bravest thing one person can do.

Section Two Questions

1. Compare and contrast the British colonization of India with the British actions in other parts of the world. How is it similar? How is it different?

2. Why is the Sepoy Rebellion considered such a turning point in India's colonial history?

3. Why is Gandhi so significant in India's history? List and support three reasons.

6.3 The Great Partition of 1947

In 1947, two countries emerged from the British colony of India: a predominantly Hindu India and a predominantly Muslim Pakistan. The middle of the country was where Hindus were dominant, whereas majorities of Muslims existed on two different sides of the country; West Pakistan became the center of government and economic activity, while East Pakistan resented their distance from the hub of activity nearly 1,000 miles away. East Pakistan officially broke away after the Bangladeshi Liberation War of 1971, and is today known as Bangladesh.

Jawaharlal Nehru and Mahatma Gandhi, 1942. Dave Davis, Acme Newspictures Inc., via the Library of Congress.

The division of the countries by religion was not clear-cut. Fourteen and a half million people ended up moving from one area of the country to another to ensure they would be in the majority.[83] Muslims fled to Pakistan; Hindus and Sikhs fled Pakistan for India. While the largest single movement of people in modern times was occurring, violence broke out between the groups in retaliation for long-simmering tensions and it was unclear what army or police force was responsible for stopping it. Some estimates put the number of dead due to the violence of the transition at one million.[84]

Though independence was a dream long-awaited for by millions of Indians, many blamed the British for the shoddy job they did of leaving the country. These critics argued that without a clear plan for the movement of millions or for who should control the area known as **Kashmir**, Britain was responsible for much of the ensuing chaos. Britain responded that their continuing presence would only add to the confusion, and that with the devastation brought by World War II, they lacked the resources to help squash the violence and preserve law and order.

Following Partition, India and Pakistan continued to maintain an openly hostile relationship, much to Gandhi's great dismay. India turned towards the USSR for assistance, while Pakistan leaned heavily (and still does today) on the US, especially on the American military.

The disputed areas between India, Pakistan and China. Map created by Planemad via Wikimedia Commons.

India has maintained a democracy apart from a short time in 1975 after Prime Minister **Indira Gandhi** (Jawaharlal Nehru's daughter and friend of Gandhi, but not related to him) declared a state of emergency. Many Indians were calling for her resignation, and she seized the opportunity to repress all political dissent. She would later be assassinated by her own Sikh bodyguards after ordering an attack on the holiest site in the Sikh religion.

Meanwhile, Pakistan has suffered numerous coups, political assassinations, and constant military domination of its political system. With the bloody history of Partition and the diametrically opposed allies, India and Pakistan ended up fighting three wars since 1947: two of which were over the disputed region of Kashmir in the north.

As we saw in Rwanda and South Africa, when a minority group rules over a majority group there can be great tension between the two. This was the case in Kashmir, ruled by a Hindu prince but with a mostly Muslim population. Still today, the claims on the territory by Pakistan and India overlap, and it is the scene of regular attacks by Muslim Kashmiris on Hindu Kashmiris and vice versa.

India and Pakistan tested nuclear weapons within weeks of each other in May 1998. The hostility that has existed between the two was ratcheted up a notch once nuclear weapons were involved, and has drawn the concern of the international community several times, though no major armed conflict between the two countries has occurred since then.

According to consultants McKinsey and Company, India has made dramatic improvements since 1994 in terms of extreme poverty. In 1994, 45 percent of Indians lived in extreme poverty; today that number is 22 percent. However, 56 percent (280 million) of Indians still lack the access to basic services that would create a decent quality of life. [85]

In 2014, India, the world's largest democracy, went to the polls to vote for members of Parliament. Of 543 seats, 282 were won by members of the Bharatiya Janata party (BJP), a pro-business, Hindu nationalist political party. In a parliamentary system, the leader of the party that has the majority of seats becomes the Prime Minister. The head of the BJP, Narendra Modi, thus became the Prime Minister. In his first two years as Prime Minister, Modi has traveled extensively abroad, trying to increase India's image as a major political and economic player on the world stage. At home, he has struggled to create the type of economic growth that will employ the 1 million Indians entering the workforce each month.[86]

How India's political and economic system will adapt to the rapid growth of its population (projected by the United Nations to overtake China's by 2022) will determine whether it can lift a massive number of Indians out of poverty and become a dominant economic rival to China.

Section Three Questions

1. What is the impact of Partition on India today? Who is to blame for the complications of the migration? India's government? Pakistan's government? Britain's government? Or was it the citizens themselves? Justify your answer in at least two paragraphs.

2. Compare and contrast India and Pakistan using at least three different variables (government, religion, population, historical identity, etc.). Feel free to use outside sources to support your answer.

GLOSSARY

Abraham: The father of the three monotheistic religions - Christianity, Islam and Judaism. According to all three religions, Abraham had a successful life in polytheistic Mesopotamia, but was told by God to move to Israel in order to spread monotheism. He was also told by God to have children, and ended up having a son, Ishmael, by his maid because his own wife, Sarah, was infertile at the time. Later, God granted Sarah fertility and Abraham had another son, Isaac, whom he was later asked to sacrifice as a test of his faith.

African National Congress: The South African political party that once fought for the end of Apartheid in South Africa and continues to be a political force in South Africa today.

African Nationalism: Pride in African countries and the idea that Africa should be ruled by Africans. Leopold Senghor is a famous example of an African nationalist.

African Union: The union of all African countries except for Morocco. It was founded in 2002 and its goal is to promote the wellbeing of all Africans.

Afrikaners: Dutch settlers in South Africa who were named after the dialect of Dutch that they spoke called Afrikaans.

Age of Exploration: A phrase referring to the 15th century, in which many "new" lands were discovered, conquered and colonized by European countries.

Ahmadinejad, Mahmoud: The president of Iran from 2005 - 2013 who presided over a period of heightened tension between Iran and the United States.

Al-Assad, Bashar: The current dictator of Syria, and son of its former leader. He has waged war on rebels since 2011, when an outbreak of protests began following the Arab Spring uprisings in other Middle Eastern countries.

Alexander the Great: The Greek liberator of the Egyptians and the conquerer of the Phoenicians. The Egyptians made him their pharaoh, and he divided his land among his top generals when he died in 336 BCE. Nearly 300 years later, Cleopatra, a descendant of one of these generals, came to power.

Ali: Muhammad's cousin and the founder of the Shia sect of Islam.

Akbar: The greatest emperor of the Mughals who took the throne at age 13. Akbar was a scholarly, although illiterate, man, and he tried very hard to unite India's Muslim and Hindu populations by marrying a Hindu princess and ending taxes on non-Muslims.

Allah: The Muslim word for the same God that Christians and Jews pray to.

Allende, Salvador: The former Socialist president of Chile who was overthrown in a US-backed coup by Auguto Pinochet in 1973.

Allied Powers of World War I: The victors of World War I that included Britain, France, Serbia, the USSR and the United States.

Allied Powers of World War II: The victors of World War II that included the United States, Britain, France, Australia, Canada and the USSR.

Al-Qaeda: The terrorist group responsible for the September 11, 2001 attacks on the US.

Amritsar Massacre: The peaceful-gathering-turned-killing of 1919 that occurred when the British army shot thousands of Sikhs for publicly gathering, which had been banned the day before. This event infuriated Indians and helped start the Indian independence movement.

Anarchism: A political system in which there is no form of government or ruling power.

Ancient Egyptian Empire: The world's longest standing empire, which survived for nearly 3,000 years. It was located in present-day Egypt and was centered around the Nile River.

Animal Farm: George Orwell's 1945 novella that was a political mockery of Stalin's rule of the USSR.

Apartheid: The period of time in South Africa's history when blacks were severely discriminated against and required to carry ID cards at all times. With the help of the African National Congress and Nelson Mandela, apartheid ended in 1994, but racism and poverty still exist in the townships where black South Africans were forced to live under the system.

Arab Spring: A series of uprisings and rebellions that began in 2010 in the Middle East and replaced dictators with new presidents. Some countries affected by the Arab Spring are Egypt, Tunisia, Libya, Syria and Yemen.

Arafat, Yasser: The name of a major Palestinian leader from the late 1960's -2004, when he died.

Aryans: The civilization of conquerors from Central Europe that brought Hinduism to India along with the caste system, Sanskrit and the Vedas. This name has also been appropriated by the Nazis to refer to people with "ideal" genes.

Ashoka: The most famous emperor of the Mughals who converted to Buddhism after he saw too much violence and pain during the Battle of Kalinga. Ashoka spread Buddhism around Asia and built Buddhist temples in India.

Assimilation:: The process of adopting a foreign culture in place of one's own.

Atahualpa: The last emperor of the Incas who killed his own brother in order to gain power. He was killed himself by Francisco Pizarro in 1532 after being kidnapped and paying a $50 million ransom.

Aurangzeb: The Mughal emperor who was the son of Shah Jahan. Aurangzeb killed his brothers and imprisoned his father for power, and was one of the last Mughal emperors.

Axis Powers of World War II: The losers of World War II that included Nazi Germany, Japan, Italy and Romania.

Ayatollah Khomeini: The religious leader of Iran who overthrew the Shah in 1979.

Aztecs: The ancient Latin American civilization that lived in present-day Mexico. They were famous for their engineering feats in the great island city of Tenochtitlan, but were conquered by Hernan Cortes in 1521.

Babur: The first Mughal emperor of India who loved reading poetry and fitness. His morning exercise was to climb up a mountain while carrying two men on his shoulders.

Babylonians: The empire that existed in Mesopotamia around 1700 BCE whose most famous ruler was Hammurabi, the author of Hammurabi's Code.

Banana Republics: The Central American countries in which the United Fruit Company was stationed to grow bananas and run the government. Many of these countries have unstable economies and political systems today.

Balfour Declaration: The British statement that allowed European Jews to move to Israel in 1917.

Bangladesh: The country that was formerly East Pakistan, which split off from West Pakistan in 1971.

Battle of Adowa, The: The battle between Italy and Ethiopia in 1896 in which the Italians were defeated handily. It stopped the Italians from trying to invade again for nearly forty years.

Bay of Pigs: The failed US military operation in which the CIA trained 1,000 Cuban exiles to invade Cuba and take the country back from Castro.

Belgian Congo: The Belgian colony of King Leopold II in which the natives were enslaved and forced to harvest rubber. The punishment for not completing the daily requirement of rubber was either beating, rape, or amputation.

Belgium: The European country that colonized the Congo, Rwanda and Burundi.

Benin: The African civilization that flourished in present-day Nigeria as a forest kingdom until well into the 1800's because of its seclusion.

Berlin Conference of 1884-1885: The meeting of thirteen nations that all came together in Berlin, Germany, to discuss the colonization of Africa and to decide which European powers deserved which territories.

Berlin Wall: The wall that separated East and West Berlin that finally came down in 1989.

Bible: The Christian holy book, split into the New and Old Testaments.

Bloody Sunday: The protest outside of the Winter Palace in St. Petersburg on January 22, 1905 that resulted in many deaths and humiliation for Tsar Nicholas II.

Bolivar, Simon: The liberator of many Latin American countries.

Bolshevik Party: Russia's Communist party that was led by Vladimir Lenin and won the Russian Civil War.

Bourgeoisie: One who is in the middle and upper class.

Boxer Rebellion: The rebellion against foreign influence in China that was led by Chinese who only fought with their fists, believing their style of fighting made them immune to bullets (it did not).

Brahmin: The highest caste in the Hindu caste system that is made up of priests.

British East India Company: The British merchant group that ruled India until 1858 and had its own army.

British Petroleum: The company that discovered oil in Iran in 1908.

British Raj: The British rule of India by the crown from 1858 - 1947.

Buddhism: The religion that believes that the key to happiness is to achieve enlightenment.

Catholicism: A form of Christianity that is the largest religion in Latin America and was brought over by conqusitadors and missionaries to the "New World".

Cape of Good Hope, The: One of the most southern points of Africa that was discovered by Bartolomeu Dias in 1488 and is now part of South Africa.

Capitalism: The economic system in which the economy and trade are controlled by private citizens and not by the government, and wages are different.

Caste System: The Hindu social system that one is born into. The highest caste one may be in is the Brahmin caste, made up of priests, followed by the Kshatriya or soldiers, Vaisya or merchants, Sudra or peasants, and Dalit, the untouchables, or the literal outcasts. Although the caste system is now illegal in India, many Hindus still use it and strive for reincarnation to a higher caste.

Central Powers of World War I: The losers of World War I that included Austria-Hungary, Germany and the Ottoman Empire.

Cheka, NKVD, KGB: The secret police of Russia, which has undergone several name changes.

Cleopatra: The famous Egyptian "pharaoh" who committed suicide after her kingdom was taken over by Octavian. She famously courted both Caesar and Marc Antony to keep power over Egypt.

Cold War: A period of tension that lasted for almost forty years between the USSR and the US and pitted communism against capitalism.

Communism: The theory that the government should control the economy and all property is held in common. In general, people will be paid the same in this system.

Cortes, Hernan: The explorer who conquered the Aztec empire in 1521 with the help of his wife/

spy La Malinche. The Aztec emperor, Moctezuma, thought he was a god.

Coup d'etat: A military takeover of the government.

Dalit: The lowest rank in India's social system ~ they are considered outside the caste system, and are literally "outcasts". Dalits are also called the untouchables and do the most unwanted work in society.

Darius the Great: The successor to Cyrus the Great who extended the Persian empire, added road, tax and postal systems and built the city of Persepolis.

De Las Casas, Bartolomé: The encomienda owner who protested the terrible treatment of the natives through the system. He appealed to Spain's monarchy and suggested they import African slaves instead, who he claimed were better suited to the climate.

Dias, Bartolomeu: The Portuguese explorer credited with the discovery of the Cape of Good Hope in 1488. He originally named it the "Cape of Storms" due to terrible weather conditions, but the King of Portugal changed it in order to make the cape sound more appealing to other explorers and future settlers.

Embargo: A complete ban on trade and commerce between countries.

Ethiopia: The only African country to resist colonization. Italy tried twice to colonize Ethiopia, but was defeated both times.

Five Pillars of Islam: The laws that devout Muslims adhere to, including declaration of faith, prayer, charity giving, fasting during Ramadan, and a pilgrimage to Mecca, Saudi Arabia.

Five Relationships: Confucius's idea that everyone should be both a ruler and the ruled. He believed that if these five relationships were followed, then society would be disciplined and would function well. They were that the ruler is greater than the ruled, the father is greater than the son, the husband is greater than the wife, the older brother is greater than the younger brother, and the friend is equal to the friend.

Five Year Plan: Stalin's plan to rapidly industrialize the USSR, which had fallen behind European countries during the Industrial Revolution. It started in 1928 and required millions of farmers to move into the cities in order to work in factories. Stalin relocated the remaining farmers into Communist collectives, which were large farms in which everything was shared. Although industrial output increased through the Five Year Plan, agricultural output decreased by 25% and 14.5 million people died of starvation. Whenever criticism was given, Stalin would make sure that his opponents either ended up in gulags or were killed by purges.

Gautama, Siddhartha: The founder of Buddhism.

Gaza Strip: The Palestinian territory that is located near Egypt and is considerably smaller than the West Bank.

Guantanamo Bay: The American military prison that is located in Cuba and was given to the US after the Spanish-American War.

Gulag: Huge labor and prison camps in which Stalin placed his "enemies of the state".

Gupta Empire: The Golden Age of India in which artistic and scientific achievements were common, expansion of the empire occurred, and war was limited.

Habyarimana, Juvenal: The president of Rwanda who was on his way to a peaceful negotiation with the Rwandan Patriotic Force when his plane was shot down in Burundi. Habyarimana died on April 6, 1994, and the group responsible for his death is still unknown.

Hammurabi: The leader of the Babylonians around 1750 BCE that wrote the oldest surviving set of laws, some of which are featured in the Louvre in Paris.

Hammurabi's Code: The world's oldest surviving set of laws that were literally set into stone by Hammurabi in the 18th century BCE. There were 282 of them and they kept the empire of Babylonia functioning with peace and discipline.

Han: The fourth dynasty of China, in which being in the government was a great honor that demanded the passing of a multi-day test. The Han also built the Silk Road, which connected China with the rest of the continent through trade.

Hijab: The veil that covers the head and chest of Muslim women.

Hinduism: The polytheistic religion that was started by the Aryans and is now followed by 80% of India. It features three main deities - the creator, Brahma, the destroyer, Shiva, and the preserver, Vishnu.

Hitler, Adolf: The dictator of Nazi Germany from 1934 to 1945 who hated Stalin yet signed the German-Soviet Non-Aggression Pact with him in 1939. He eventually went back on his promise and attacked the Soviet Union during Operation Barbarossa, and is the muse for the character Mr. Frederick in Animal Farm.

Hittites: Conquerors of Mesopotamia and Turkey in the 18th century BCE.

Homo Sapiens: The scientific name for common-day humans, which first evolved in Africa 100,000 years ago.

Hutu: The made-up ethnic group that murdered 1 million Tutsis in the Rwandan Genocide.

Isaac: The son of Abraham and Sarah, and the father of the Jews.

Ishmael: The son of Abraham and his maid Hagar, and the father of the Muslims.

Islam: A monotheistic religion that believes in the Five Pillars and is the dominant religion throughout the Middle East, North Africa, and parts of South Asia.

Italy: The European nation that successfully colonized Libya, Eritrea and Somalia but failed to colonize Ethiopia. Italy was defeated by Ethiopia in 1896 and then again in 1935, making Ethiopia the only African country to resist colonization.

Jinnah, Muhammad Ali: An activist for the Indian Independence Movement who was the first prime minister of Pakistan.

Judaism: A monotheistic religion that believes in the Old Testament of the Bible.

Kai-Shek, Chiang: The leader of the Chinese Nationalist Party.

Kerensky, Alexander: The head of Russia's Provisional Government, which lasted for only ten months and was overtaken bloodlessly by the Bolsheviks during the October Revolution.

Kshatriya: The second highest caste in the caste system, which is made up of soldiers.

Kulaks: The names for the wealthy Russian peasants that were reluctant to collectivize and were killed by Stalin. They were represented by the chickens in George Orwell's book *Animal Farm*.

Kush: An ancient African civilization that flourished from 1070 BC to 350 AD in modern-day Sudan, but was unfortunately washed away by a collapsing dam after being conquered by the Romans.

La Malinche: The wife of Hernan Cortes and a spy who betrayed the Aztecs in order to help the conquistadors. Her children were the first mestizo, or mixed, people in Latin America.

Lao Tse: The founder of Taoism.

Land Reform: The act of taking land from the rich and distributing it among the poor.

Lenin, Vladimir: The leader of the Bolshevik party and first leader of the USSR who disliked Stalin and thought that he was "rude." Lenin died in 1924.

Liberia: America's only African colony in which freed slaves were returned to their home continent. Tensions between Americo-Liberians and native Liberians led to a civil war.

L'Ouverture, Toussaint: The liberator of Haiti from French rule.

Maasai: A nomadic ethnic group that lives in Kenya and raises cows.

Mali: The wealthy ancient African empire that was located in western Africa.

Mandela, Nelson: Anti-apartheid activist and South Africa's first democratically-elected president.

Mansa Musa: The famous king of Mali who traveled all around Africa on a pilgrimage and threw so much gold into the streets in Cairo that its price fell for twenty years.

Martyrdom: The act of giving one's life for a cause or as a sacrifice.

Marxism: A political and economic theory created by Karl Marx in which the proletariats overthrow the bourgeoisie.

Mau Mau Rebellion: a rebellion of Kikuyu Kenyans against the ruling British colonial powers. Britain eventually put down the rebellion with thousands of Kikuyu deaths.

Mayas: The oldest of Latin America's pre-Colombian civilizations that was centered in Guatemala. The Mayans created the 365.25 day calendar, used city-states, and played a game in which the losing team was sacrificed to the gods. The Mayans were not conquered; they mysteriously disappeared around 300 BCE.

Medvedev, Dmitri: The president of Russia from 2008 - 2012 who was replaced by Vladimir Putin.

Menes: The first pharaoh, or king, of Egypt. He united Upper and Lower Egypt around 3100 BCE.

Mexican-American War: The war between Mexico and America from 1846 - 1848 that resulted in the US gaining the modern-day states of Utah, California, Nevada, New Mexico, Colorado, Oklahoma, Arizona, Wyoming and Texas and paying Mexico $15 million in compensation.

Modi: India's current Prime Minister, elected 2014. A member of the Hindu nationalist BJP party.

Monotheism: The belief that there is only one god, which includes the religions of Christianity, Islam and Judaism.

Monroe Doctrine: The United States declaration that the "Western Hemisphere shall henceforth not be considered subjects for European colonization."

Mountbatten Plan: The formal name for the British plan to split India and Pakistan by religion.

Mughals: The last Indian empire - also known as the Mongols - that ruled from 1526 - 1858. It was a Muslim empire and contained emperors such as Babur, Akbar, Shah Jahan and Aurangzeb.

Muhammad: The prophet that started the religion of Islam in the year 622 AD.

Mummification: The ancient Egyptian process of preserving the kings' bodies so that they could keep them during the afterlife. The four "most important" organs - intestines, stomach, lungs and liver - were placed in canopic jars while the brain was taken out through the nose using a long hook and then thrown away. The process took almost two months and has several gods associated with it. Because of mummification and its relation to the Egyptians' ideas of the afterlife, archaeologists are now able to understand much of what daily life was like.

Nationalism: A strong pride in one's nation, often as the most important part of one's identity.

One-Party Rule: The form of government where there is only one political party within a country.

Pan-Africanism: The belief in uniting Africa as one nation, celebrating the kinship of all Africans.

Pinochet, Augusto: The former dictator of Chile accused of crimes against humanity and put on trial in Britain in 1998 but not convicted of anything. Pinochet was good friends with British prime minister Margaret Thatcher and, although he killed thousands of people, some scholars argue that he massively improved Chile's economy.

Pizarro, Francisco: The conqueror of the Incas that killed Atahualpa in 1532.

Pope Urban II: The pope that authorized the beginning of the Crusades.

Portugal: A European country that colonized several countries in Africa and Brazil in Latin America.

Pravda: The Soviet propaganda newspaper, whose name means "Truth".

Pre-Columbian Latin America: The name for Latin America before Columbus landed in 1492, which included the civilizations of the Mayas, Incas and Aztecs.

Pre-History: The period of time before history was able to be written down and instead had to be passed down orally from one generation to the next.

Propaganda: Information, usually false, that is used either to promote or hurt a political cause.

Provisional Government of Russia: The government that was made up of former members of the Duma and headed by Alexander Kerensky. It was overthrown by the Bolsheviks in October of 1917 after only ten months.

Puerto Rico: An American territory in the Caribbean that may one day become the 51st state and that was gained by the US after winning the Spanish-American War.

Putin, Vladimir: The name of Russia's current president, its prime minister from 2008 - 2012, its president from 2000 - 2008 and the former head of the KGB, or Russian police.

Qin: The third dynasty of China which was the first to unite China and under which the Great Wall was built.

Qin Shi Huangdi: China's first emperor and namesake. Huangdi began construction on the Great Wall, drank mercury in search of immortality, and built his own army of terracotta soldiers to guard him in death.

Qing: The final Chinese dynasty. Fell due to Boxer Rebellion, Opium war, Open Door Policy, spheres of influence, Taiping Rebellion, Empress Ci Xi, and the failure of the 100 Days of Reform.

Queen Isabella: The queen of Spain in the 15th century who sent conquistadors like Christopher Columbus over to the New World in search of gold and other prizes.

Queen Victoria: The queen of Britain in the 19th century who called herself "Empress of India".

Quran: The Muslim holy book.

Rabin, Yitzhak: The former Israeli prime minister who was assassinated by an Israeli student in 1995 after signing the Oslo Accords.

Red Army: The Bolshevik army that won the Russian civil war of 1917 - 1922. The Red Army was led by brilliant Leon Trotsky, who kept the men optimistic, hygienic and ready to fight.

Romanov, Tsar Nicholas II: The aloof and family-oriented last tsar, or king, of Russia. Although protests occurred during his reign, Nicholas II was more interested in himself, and was finally forced to abdicate in February of 1917.

Romanov, Tsarevich Alexei: The son of Tsar Nicholas II and Tsarina Alexandra who was a hemophiliac and demanded the medical attention of Grigori Rasputin, whom his mother had an affair with. Alexei was murdered along with his four sisters and parents on July 17, 1918.

Romanov ,Tsarina Alexandra: The wife of Tsar Nicholas II of Russia, who had five children and had an affair with her son Alexei's mystical "doctor", Rasputin.

Roosevelt, Teddy: The former Secretary of the US Navy and leader of a group of calvarymen during the Spanish-American War called "Rough Riders". Roosevelt also convinced the US to go to war with Spain, put in place the project to build the Panama Canal, and became the 26th president of the US.

Russian Civil War: A war fought from 1917 - 1922 between the Bolshevik Army and the White

Army.

Rwandan Genocide: The killing of Tutsis and moderate Hutus by extremist Hutus of the Interhamwe and Hutu Army over the period of 100 days in 1994 in the country of Rwanda. The massacres began after the plane that Rwanda's Hutu president was flying in was shot down. The United Nations withdrew most of their peacekeepers and the United States refused to get invovled due to the recent disaster in Somalia.

Salt March: A 200-mile long March to the Sea led by Gandhi in a protest against British taxes on salt.

Sanskrit: The ancient Aryan language that the Vedas are written in.

Sanctions: a ban or limit on types of trade, usually not as complete as an embargo.

Sarah: Abraham's wife, who graciously let her husband have a child with the maid due to her own infertility. After thirteen years, God granted her the ability to reproduce and she had a son, Issac, who grew to be the father of the Christians and Jews.

Satyagraha: Gandhi's political ideal that included devotion to the truth and nonviolence.

SAVAK: The name for Shah Pahlavi's secret police force that was trained by the CIA and repressed any opponents of the Shah's rule.

Sepoy: The name for an Indian soldier in the British army from the region of Bengal.

Sepoy Rebellion: The 1857 rebellion that started when sepoys in Cawnpore murdered their British officers. To retaliate, the British tied sepoys to cannons and then fired them. The Sepoy Rebellion changed India by increasing tension between Muslims and Hindus and between the Indians and the British, transferring control over India from the British East India Company to the British crown, and ending the reign of the Mughal empire.

Shah: The former name for the king of Iran.

Shah Jahan: The Mughal emperor who built the Taj Mahal.

Shang: The first dynasty of China, which is famous for creating a writing system.

Shia: The sect of Islam that believed the next ruler after Mohammad should have been directly related to him.

Sikhism: The religion that is a mixture of Islam and Hinduism that believes in reincarnation but only one god.

Six Day War: A six-day long war fought in 1967 between Israel and countries supportive of Palestine.

Socialism: An economic system in which the government has some control over the economy, but property is not held in common.

Song: The seventh dynasty of China during which rice replaced wheat, tea replaced wine, upturned roofs became popular and foot binding began.

Songhay: The southern-African ancient empire that contained the scholarly city of Timbuktu.

Spain: The European colonial power that colonized many countries in Latin America.

Spanish-American War: The war fought in 1898 between Spain and the US over Cuba. For winning, the United States received the territories of Puerto Rico, Guam and the Philippines, an ability to intervene in Cuba's affairs, and a permanent military base in Cuba called Guantanamo Bay.

Spheres of Influence: The division of China into certain parts that were controlled by the colonial powers of Austria, France, Germany, Great Britain, Italy, Japan and Russia.

Sputnik: The first satellite that was launched by the Russians.

Stanley, Henry Morton: A reporter for the *New York Herald* who was sent to Africa to find Dr. David Livingstone. Stanley found him in 1871 in Ujiji, present-day Tanzania, and asked him, "Dr. Livingstone, I presume?" Stanley then abandoned his job as a reporter and became a famous explorer, traveling around Africa and even claiming the Congo for Belgium's King Leopold II.

Sudra: The lowest and largest caste in the caste system that contains peasants.

Sui: The fifth dynasty of China that used Legalist tactics to reunite the empire after a chaotic period.

Suleiman the Magnificent: An Ottoman emperor.

Sumerians: An ancient Mesopotamian empire.

Sunni: The type of Islam that believed that the next leader after Mohammed should have been the best Muslim.

Sykes-Picot Agreement: A secret pact between Britain and france to divide the Ottoman Empire between themselves following the victory in WWI. It set the modern country borders for the region.

Taiping Rebellion: The rebellion of Christians against the Qing dynasty that killed 20 million and weakened the public's faith in the Qing.

Taj Mahal: The famous Indian masoleum built by Mughal emperor Shah Jahan to honor his wife, who died giving birth to their fourteenth child.

Tang: The sixth dynasty of China during which the Golden Age of China took place.

Taoism: The Chinese school of philosophy that states that humans should not interefere with nature's way.

Tiananmen Square: The famous square in which college students gathered in 1989 to protest Communism and to ask for more democracy. The students would not leave, and after six weeks, tanks from the Chinese Army rolled in to clear the square and ended up killing thousands of people in the process. This massacre was a sign to the rest of the world that China still had a long way to go to reach democracy.

Timbuktu: The scholarly capital of the ancient African empire of Songhay.

Torah: The Jewish holy book, or the Old Testament of the Bible.

Totalitarianism: The political system in which a government is a single party dictatorship and controls nearly everything about its citizens' daily lives. North Korea is an example of totalitarian rule.

Townships: Slums that black South Africans were forced to live in during apartheid. Many blacks still live in these neighborhoods today.

Treaty of Guadalupe Hidalgo: The treaty signed between the US and Mexico that formally ended the Mexican-American War and gave the US the modern-day states of Utah, California, Nevada, New Mexico, Colorado, Oklahoma, Arizona, Wyoming and Texas and $15 million in compensation.

Treaty of Nanjing: The treaty signed between the Chinese and the British in 1842 that ended the Opium War, gave Britain five Chinese ports to use, gave British politicians extraterritoriality, and demanded a large fine from China.

Treaty of the Sevres: The treaty signed by the Ottoman Empire in 1917 that ended its involvement in World War I and gave Britain and France the territories of Syria, Lebanon, Iraq, Jordan, Palestine and Kuwait.

Treaty of Tordesillas: The treaty signed between Spain and Portugal that was signed in 1494. It gave Portugal the right to colonize Brazil, and let Spain colonize whatever remained of Latin America.

Tutankhamun: The famed boy-king of Egypt whose mummy was found intact by archeologist Howard Carter in 1922. Tutankhamun's tomb has led archaeologists to understand more about daily life in ancient Egypt and has fascinated the public because of the many riches and treasures associated with it.

Tutsi: The ethnic group created by the Belgians that contained the taller, thinner Africans. The Belgians claimed that they looked more "European", and put them in positions of power. Over 1 million Tutsi died during the Rwandan Genocide, in which they were targeted by the Hutu.

Ujiji: The village in which David Livingstone was found in 1871 by Henry Morton Stanley and asked the famous question, "Dr. Livingstone, I presume?"

United Fruit Company: The American fruit company that took over the governments of Central American countries in order to grow bananas. The UFC only grew a few types of banana, so when a strange disease hit, it wiped out all of the bananas and led to the extinction of the largest, sweetest type of banana.

United Nations: The international organization of countries that was created in 1945 to promote peace and security.

United Nations Resolution 181: The agreement made by the United Nations in 1947 that split the land of what was formerly known as British Palestine into Israel (55% of the land) and Palestine (45% of the land) and made Jerusalem an international city. This led to an Arab-Israeli War in 1948.

Union of Soviet Socialist Republics: The formal name of the USSR, which lasted from 1922 to 1991 and contained fifteen countries including Russia.

Vaisya: The third highest caste in the Hindu caste system, which is made up of merchants.

Vedas: The oldest of the Hindu holy books.

Von Bismarck, Otto: A German politician who headed the Berlin Conference of 1884 - 1885 in order to carve up "the magnificent African cake."

West Bank: The Palestinian territory that is located near Jordan on the West Bank of the Jordan River and contains half of the city of Jerusalem.

White Army: The army that lost the Russian Civil War of 1917 - 1922. The White Army was not well disciplined or well organized, and it was defeated by the Bolshevik, or Red, Army.

White Man's Burden, The: The racist idea that it is the duty of the white man to educate the Africans, civilize them and teach them Christianity.

Winter Palace: The setting for the January 22, 1905 massacre of Bloody Sunday and the headquarters of the Russian Provisional Government. The Winter Palace can still be toured today in St. Petersburg, Russia.

World War I: A large-scale war fought from 1914 - 1918 between the Allied and Central Powers.

World War II: A large-scale war fought from 1939 - 1945 between the Allied and Axis Powers.

Xenophile: One who loves foreign things. Xenophiles were targeted by Mao during his Cultural Revolution.

Xhosa: The native people that the Dutch came into contact with when they colonized South Africa in the 17th century. Countless wars were fought between the two groups, and the Dutch ended up taking most of the Xhosa's land for farming and agriculture.

Xiaoping, Deng: The successor to Mao Zedong who opened up the economy, calling it "socialism with Chinese character" and ordered the clearing of Tiananmen Square.

Year of Africa, The: The nickname for 1960 because of the seventeen African countries that gained independence that year.

Yuan: The eighth dynasty of China that was ruled by the Mongols and led by Genghis Khan's grandson. This dynasty is the namesake of the modern-day currency of China.

Zhou: The second dynasty of China, which is credited with the invention of the Mandate of Heaven.

Ziggurat: The Sumerian name for a temple, which was similar to that of the Egyptians.

Zimbabwe: The southern-African empire that created large stone structures and traded ivory, gold and copper with the Swahili people of eastern Africa.

Zionists: A group that was created in the early 20th century by European Jews who wanted to return to their "Promised Land" of Israel.

Acknowledgements

All images in this book were either collected from the public domain, creative commons, or the author's own work, and all available information regarding sources, authors, and dates are noted in the captions. Most of these images are in the public domain due to expired copyrights in the United States, Russia, India, Britain and China. For more information on public domain photos, check out the Flickr Creative Commons project or the Wikimedia Commons Foundation. I am deeply indebted to these two resources for the images in this book.

The cover image is by Geraint Rowland, "All alone in Mexico City", August 30, 2012 via Flickr Creative Commons and direct consent from the author.

Thank you Nick Zosel-Johnson, Alan and Nancy Sparrow, Brianna Showalter, Rudy Ford, Dr. David Adams, Rob Scotlan, Lydia Roberts, Julianna Sparrow, Piper Coyner, Trevor Gagnier, Nolan Roberts, Paige Brink and Brooke Brakke Judge for your help and support on this project.

Russia

1   Hasic, Albinko. "Rasputin: 5 Myths and Truths About the Mystic Russian Monk." *Time*, 29 Dec. 2016.

2   Engelstein, Laura. "Revolution of 1905 (Russia)." Europe 1789-1914: Encyclopedia of the Age of Industry and Empire, edited by John Merriman and Jay Winter, vol. 4, Charles Scribner's Sons, 2006, pp. 1974-1979.

3   Ibid.

4   Ascher, Abraham. The Revolution of 1905. Stanford, Calif.: Stanford UP, 1988. p. 91.

5   Montefiore, Simon Sebag .*Young Stalin*. London: Weidenfeld & Nicolson, 2007.

6   Montefiore, Simon Sebag "Stalin." *New York Times*.18 Apr. 2004.

7   Rabinowitch, Alexander. The Bolsheviks Come to Power: The Revolution of 1917 in Petrograd. Pluto Press. pp. 273–305.

8   "Russian Civil War." Europe Since 1914: Encyclopedia of the Age of War and Reconstruction, edited by John Merriman and Jay Winter, vol. 4, Charles Scribner's Sons, 2006, pp. 2267-2272.

9   Gunther, John. *Inside Europe*. Harper & Brothers. 1940.

10   Mansky, Jackie. "The True Story Of The Death Of Stalin." *Smithsonian*. 2017.

11   Laub, Zachary. "The Taliban In Afghanistan." Council on Foreign Relations. 2018.

12   "Putin won 'rigged elections'". BBC News. 11 September 2000.

13   Yourish, Karen, and Troy Griggs. "Trump Trusts Putin's Denial, But Seven U.S. Intelligence Groups Blame Russia For Election Meddling." Nytimes.com. 17 July 2018.

Africa

14   "Mummification." World Eras, edited by Edward I. Bleiberg, vol. 5: Ancient Egypt, 2615 - 332 B.C.E. Gale, 2002, pp. 281-283. World History In Context.

15   Ibid.

16   "Menes: King Of Egypt." Encyclopedia Britannica. 2018.

17   Crawford, Amy. "Who Was Cleopatra?." *Smithsonian*. 31 Mar 2007.

18   Burstein, Stanley M. *The Reign of Cleopatra*. Greenwood Pres, 2004,Westport, CT.

19   Gray, Melissa. "Poison, not snake, killed Cleopatra, scholar says - Cleopatra died a quiet and pain free death, historian alleges". CNN. 30 June 2010.

20   Morgan, Thad."This 14th-Century African Emperor Remains The Richest Person In History." History. A & E Networks.

21   Onishi, Norimitsu. "Zimbabwe's Rulers Use A Monument's Walls To Build A Legacy." Nytimes.com. 21 Feb 2017.

22   "Bartolomeu Dias." History.com. A & E Networks. 2009.

23   Ibid.

24   Valsecchi, Pierluigi. *Power and State Formation in West Africa*. Springer, 2011.

25   "Exploration of the Nile River: A Journey of Discovery and Imperialism." Science and Its Times, edited by Neil Schlager and Josh Lauer, vol. 5, Gale, 2001.

26   Sterling, Thomas. *Into Africa*. New Word City, 2016.

27   "David Livingstone Traverses the African Continent." Science and Its Times, edited by

Neil Schlager and Josh Lauer, vol. 5, Gale, 2001.

28   Thomas Pakenham, *The Scramble for Africa: White Man's Conquest of the Dark Continent From 1876 to 1912*, New York: Avon Books, 1992.

29   Ibid.

30   "Africa: French Colonies." *Encyclopedia of Race and Racism*, edited by John Hartwell Moore, vol. 1, Macmillan Reference USA, 2008, pp. 28-34.

31   Mcgreal, Chris. "Shameful Legacy." *The Guardian*. 13 Oct 2006.

32   Hochschild, Adam. *King Leopold's Ghost: A Story Of Greed, Terror, And Heroism In Colonial Africa*. Boston : Houghton Mifflin, 1998. Print.

33   Mwanamilongo, Saleh. "Africa In World War II: The Forgotten Veterans." DW. 7 May 2015.

34   Kazeem, Yomi. "What Is A Coup? These 40 African Countries Could Help Explain." Quartz. 16 November 2017.

35   de Quevette, Harry. "Mitterand 'Knew Of Torture In Algeria.'" *Telegraph.co.uk*. 3 May 2001.

36   Ajami, Fouad. "The Furrows of Algeria". *New Republic*. 27 January 2010.

37   Gerard, Emmanuel and Kuklick, Bruce. *Death in the Congo: Murdering Patrice Lumumba*. Cambridge, MA: Harvard University Press, 2015.

38   Hancock, W.K. *Smuts I: The Sanguine Years 1870–1919*, Cambridge University Press, 1962

39   "Genocide in Rwanda." *Encyclopedia of Race and Racism*, edited by John Hartwell Moore, vol. 2, Macmillan Reference USA, 2008, pp. 52-59.

Middle East

40   "Hammurabi." Historic World Leaders, edited by Anne Commire, Gale, 1994.

41   "Mapping The Global Muslim Population." Pew Research Center's Religion & Public Life Project. 7 Oct 2009.

42   Russell, Frederick H. "Crusade, Children's." Dictionary of the Middle Ages, edited by Joseph R. Strayer, Charles Scribner's Sons, 1989.

43   "General Progress Report and Supplementary Report of the United Nations Conciliation Commission for Palestine, Covering the Period from 11 December 1949 to 23 October 1950". United Nations Conciliation Commission for Palestine. 1950.

44   Tessler, Mark. *A History of the Israeli–Palestinian Conflict*. Indiana, 1994..

45   Dehghan, Saeed and Norton-Taylor, Richard. "CIA admits role in 1953 Iranian coup". *The Guardian*.19 August 2013.

46   Gladstone, Rick. "Iran Takes U.S. To Court Over Nuclear Deal And Reimposed Sanctions." Nytimes.com. 17 July 2018.

47   Calderwood, James. "Kuwait May Write Off Billions In Loans To Iraq." *The National*. 19 Jan 2010.

48   Bump, Phillip. "15 Years After Iraq War Began, Death Toll Still Murky." *Washington Post*. 20 March 2018.

49   Hirst, David."Colonel Muammar Gaddafi obituary." *The Guardian*. 20 Oct 2011.

Latin America

50   Archibold, Randal. "Doomsday Fizzles, But Many In Old Mayan Empire Hail New Era." Nytimes.com. 21 Dec 2012.

51   Cline, Sarah. "Aztecs." Encyclopedia of Genocide and Crimes Against Humanity, edited by

Dinah L. Shelton, vol. 1, Macmillan Reference USA, 2005, pp. 104-107.

52   Hemming, John. *The Conquest of the Incas.* London: Macmillan, 1993.

53   Newson, Linda. "Pathogens, Places and Peoples." *Technology, Disease and Colonial Conquests, Sixteenth to Eighteenth Centuries,* ed.George Raudzens, 167-210. Brill, 2001.

54   "China Beat Columbus To It, Perhaps." *The Economist.* 12 Jan 2006.

55   "Christopher Columbus " History.com. 2018. A & E Networks.

56   Archer, Christon I. "Hidalgo y Costilla, Miguel (1753–1811)." *Encyclopedia of Latin American History and Culture,* edited by Jay Kinsbruner and Erick D. Langer, 2nd ed., vol. 3, Charles Scribner's Sons, 2008, pp. 687-689.

57   Ibid.

58   Liss, Peggy and Liss, Sheldon. *Man, State, and Society in Latin American History.* Praeger, 1972.

59   "The USS Maine Sinks: February 15, 1898." Global Events: Milestone Events Throughout History, edited by Jennifer Stock, vol. 6: North America, Gale, 2014.

60   "Destruction Of USS Maine." History.navy.mil. 2018.

61   "Building the Panama Canal" Office Of The Historian. History.state.gov. 2018.

62   "TR And The Panama Canal" Pbs.org. 2018.

63   Ibid.

64   "Castro's Failed Coup ." Pbs.org. 2018.

65   Campbell, Duncan. "638 Ways To Kill Castro." *The Guardian.* 2 Aug 2006.

66   "As Catholicism Declines In Latin America And U.S., Parishes Still Count On Latino Growth." NBC News. 27 May 2018.

China

67   Xiaoping, Deng "Building Socialism with a Specifically Chinese Character". Peoples Daily. 1 October 1984.

68   Wright, David Curtis. *The History of China.* Greenwood Publishing Group, 2001 p. 49.

69   Portal, Jane. *The First Emperor: China's Terracotta Army.* Harvard University Press, 2007.

70   Melancon, Glenn. "Honor in Opium? The British Declaration of War on China, 1839-1840", *International History Review,* 1999, p. 859.

71   "Long March." Britannica School, *Encyclopædia Britannica,* 2 May. 2014.

72   Bernstein, Richard. "Was Life Better Before Mao's Revolution?" Nytimes.com. 30 Oct 1983.

73   "Rural Development, 1949–1978: Great Leap Forward." *Encyclopedia of Modern China,* edited by David Pong, vol. 3, Charles Scribner's Sons, 2009, pp. 304-307.

74   Ibid.

75   Cheng, Kris. "Declassified: Chinese official said at least 10,000 civilians died in 1989 Tiananmen massacre, documents show". *Hong Kong Free Press.* 21 December 2017.

India

76   Hiro, Dilip. "Love Poems, Memoirs and Massacres the Emperor Babur was a Statesman, a General - and a Literary Master in Two Languages, Says Dilip Hiro." *The Daily Telegraph,* 24 Mar 2007, pp. 011.

77   John, L. E. "Akbar, Jalaludin Muhammad." Oxford University Press, UK, Oxford, 2004.

78   Fenech, Louis E. and McLeod, W.H. *Historical Dictionary of Sikhism*. Rowman & Littlefield Publishers, 2014.

79   "The Sepoy Rebellion: May 10, 1857–June 1858." Global Events: Milestone Events Throughout History, edited by Jennifer Stock, vol. 2: Asia and Oceania, *Gale*, 2014. Bryant, Mark.

80   "Britannia's Victorian War artist: Mark Bryant looks at the work of the Punch artist whose drawings symbolized British anger over the Indian Mutiny and established his own reputation." *History Today*, May 2007, p. 58.

81   "The Sepoy Rebellion: May 10, 1857–June 1858." Global Events: Milestone Events Throughout History, edited by Jennifer Stock, vol. 2: Asia and Oceania, *Gale*, 2014. Bryant, Mark.

82   Ives, Susan. "Gandhi's Salt March Holds Lessons For Today." *South Florida Sun - Sentinel*, Apr 21, 2004, pp. 23A.

83   *Population Redistribution and Development in South Asia*. Springer Science & Business Media. 2012. p. 6.

84   "India Gains Independence from Great Britain: August 15, 1947." Global Events: Milestone Events Throughout History, edited by Jennifer Stock, vol. 2: Asia and Oceania, *Gale*, 2014.

85   Gupta, Rajat, Shirish Sankhe, Richard Dobbs, Jonathan Woetzel, Anu Madgavkar, and Ashwin Hasyagar. "India's Path from Poverty to Empowerment." McKinsey & Company. Feb 2014.

86   Bhattacharya, Sidhu. "A Million Indians Reach Employable Age Each Month: More Jobs, Better Jobs' Data Needed" *Firstpost*. 21 Apr 2016.

Made in the USA
Monee, IL
25 July 2020